MW01519233

STONE'S

ROCK

BOTTOM

Donald R. Frye, Jr.

TJG Management Publishing, Inc. – Nevada

Library of Congress Control No: 2011939403

ISBN: 978-0-9762347-9-1

Published by: TJG Management Services

Edited by: Mychal Oliver

Cover Design by: Donald R. Frye, Jr.

STONE'S ROCK BOTTOM

**ALL ARTWORK IN THIS BOOK IS
ILLUSTRATED BY DONALD R. FRYE**

CONTENTS

Dedicated in Loving memory of my mother
Rosetta E. Frye and my brother Ramon G. Frye.

I love you mom and brother and miss you both
immensely.

DEDICATED TO

Ann Frye
Monique and Marlene Frye
Echo and Azure Frye
Anthony, Theresa, and Ronald Gonsalves
Tanya and Sheila Howard
Lynell and Jeffery
All the rest of my family

SPECIAL THANKS

To my daughter Marlene who continued to believe in me. It is because of YOU that this story was able to be written. I love you Marlene and you are the best daughter a dad could possibly ask for.

APOLOGIES:

Goody, Monique and Marlene I apologize for doing our family wrong. Please find it in your heart to forgive me.

To all of those who have been negatively impacted by my actions – I apologize.

FOREWORD

I begin by thanking my higher power whom I choose to call God.

Secondly, I thank those who were instrumental in paving the roads to recovery like AA's co-founders Bill W. and Dr. Bob, and the many women and men who shared their experiences, strengths, and hopes.

They have given me comfort and guidance while I traveled down those same desperate and lonely roads.

I boisterously applaud all who are in recovery and I continuously reach out to the addict and alcoholic who are still out there sick and suffering. I've grown to consider you all as my family. So, if no one has told you today that they love you, well … I love you.

For me, recovery's greatest attributes are those idioms that we speak on a daily basis such as:

Keep coming back.

It works, if you work it.

One day at time.

Just for today.

All will be well.

And my favorite heartfelt serenity prayer:

> *"God grant us the serenity to accept the things we cannot change, courage to change the things we cannot change, courage to change the things we can, and the wisdom to know the difference."*

The unity created amongst the groups is parallel to none and is certainly a main contributing factor with helping me to stay clean and sober today.

Writing this story was extremely difficult for me because I was compelled to search deep within my conscience to locate and expose my true character, the person I have been hiding from to an entire world.

This project was necessary gain for me. Please make yourself comfortable and enjoy this easy read. Try not to compare our experiences but discover those identifying marks which bind us together. Use them as an educational and inspirational stepping stone to a greater, more prosperous future for you and your loved ones. Most importantly, keep coming back because *"it works ... if you work it."*

Donald R. Frye, Jr.

WHAT IS ADDICTION?

It is very well documented and debated within the psychological and sober circles that addiction is a disease of the mind. Substance abuse is just one of the underlying symptoms of this destructive disease.

For example, symptoms of addiction include an overabundance of gambling, sex, work, and eating, to name a few, to the extent that they become self-destructive.

Relying on my own personal experiences, rather than deal with life on life's own terms, I, the alcoholic and drug addict, resorted to mind altering substances in order to suppress or evade my true often hurtful feelings regarding specific events at various stages of my development.

Events such as child or spousal abuse, rape, loss of close relative or friend, feelings of insecurity about myself or my relationships, abandonment, rejection, social and economic status, and loss of employment, are subjects that I had no control over (outside cues).

Instead of dealing with these issues sober and on life's terms, I tended to self-medicate using mind altering substances.

Once I self-medicated, the alcohol and drugs, took control of my thoughts. Instantly I became dependent on the continued use of them to make me feel normal or to get me through those fearful anxiety filled moments.

These behaviors compounded my problems and then led me on an endless spiral of self-destruction for over twenty years.

It doesn't have to be that way for you.

Donald R. Frye, Jr.

WHO AM I?

My name is Donald, also known as "Stone." I'm the kind of stone that rolls but gathers no moss. It is by the good grace of God that today I am a grateful and productive recovering substance abuser.

This tragic, yet now liberating, story will take your mind on a journey that reaches to the depths of despair where my cunning addiction dragged me and then led me to the victories down the road to my recovery.

The idea for this liberating project was inspired, by a spiritually transforming moment in my life.

This was a time when the juices of my brain were stewing in one hundred and five degree temperatures while being caged in solitary confinement - a lonely, damp, rodent, insect infested isolation cell obscured within the thirty-five foot reinforced concrete walls of the Massachusetts Correction Institution at Norfolk– a Massachusetts state penitentiary. MCI-Norfolk is widely known as one of this country's most psychologically and sadistically punishing institutions.

Eleven years prior to my spiritually transforming moment, I shockingly found myself incarcerated, remorsefully serving a sixteen year prison sentence for the murder of my biological brother, Ramon.

Ramon and I were both substance abusers. We often physically fought while under the influence of alcohol or drugs. My brother's demise marked the beginning of the end of our addictions, jails, institutions and any other horrific events controlling our semblance of what we called living.

While serving time in solitary confinement, I spent plenty of my time reflecting before I made a conscious decision to share my experiences, strengths and hopes with the entire world hoping to educate the hearts and minds of all who are affected by the dreadful disease of alcohol and drug addiction either directly or indirectly through a loved one, stranger, or friend.

Besides noticing the desperate tones of the other unfortunate souls who occupied the surrounding steel cage, other disturbances danced in my head of hauntingly painful memories that constantly plagued my mind. They were the cringing cries of the countless victims whom I left behind, scarred for life.

One particular solitary evening, I felt the increasing agonizing pain of the alcoholics and drug addicts who were still out there sick and slowly suffering. Instantly, it became my emotional anthem of freedom and hope.

The culmination of my masterful thoughts sent streams of energy through my aching brittle bones giving me a whole new outlook on life which caused me to share this liberating treasure, <u>Stone's Rock Bottom</u>.

At the time of starting this story, I was gratefully claiming eleven years clean and sober.

After two degrading decades of constantly abusing mind altering substances, my body and soul had grown extremely toxic. I cannot pinpoint the day or moment that I actually became sober. However, I can fervently tell you about my last time using. It was on the tragic night of July 30, 1996.

This is the last time I saw my brother alive. Earlier that day, I had consumed approximately one pint of Smirnoff Vodka and inhaled approximately one hundred dollars of crack cocaine. When I woke from the stupor, my brother was dead and I was sitting in the county jail being held responsible for his death.

Throughout my journey, I've discovered that in order to maintain my sobriety, I had to completely give of myself, by openly sharing my experiences, strengths, and hopes. I've accomplished that task. I accomplished it with a no-holds-barred confession of my innermost and deepest darkest encounters before, during, and after my twenty years of abusing mind altering substances.

I pray that these truths set me free.

Some of the proceeds from the sale of this book will benefit some of the tens of thousands of clean and sober programs which permeate this country and around the globe. Many of these programs are operated by recovering alcoholics and addicts who continue to live sober one day at a time with the desire to help others to stay clean.

"One addict or alcoholic helping another is without parallel."

Chapter

One

FALLIBLE

I was born into this world an innocent child on September 2, 1962. Nothing would prepare my family, or even society for the horrific transformations I would undergo throughout my upbringing - an upbringing, on the dangerous, drug-infested streets of Boston, Massachusetts.

I am the youngest of five siblings, four boys and one girl. By the time I reached four years old, our mother, who shared a classy and elegant resemblance to her two favorite performers, Dionne Warwick and Nancy Wilson, had removed herself from a mentally and physically abusive marriage to my father, Donald Frye Sr. whose name I have garnered all my life.

Our father is a Korean War marine veteran who suffers from post-traumatic stress disorder and could have used some medication to control his moods. At that time, I was only a small child unable to understand the events that were taking place. Still, to this very day, my mind is plagued with their loud, scary arguments and the shattering of glass that emanated from the constant bouts in which our mother was badly beaten. Luckily she was courageous enough to one day move us out of that apartment while our father was away at work.

We moved into a high-rise in the Columbia Point housing projects next to the infamous city of South Boston. During the sixties, this area was notoriously known for gang and drug activity. Once we got settled, my mother, Rosetta Frye, began drinking socially with her friends.

In the beginning, she was a functioning drinker who managed to hold down two jobs in order to support us all. She was a beautiful, intelligent, black woman who had the strong desire to succeed in life and had ambitions to move us up out of those unhealthy projects as soon as her paycheck would permit.

When mother wasn't working at the bank, she would work as a seamstress, sewing clothes, or performing other menial jobs on the weekends. Her down time was spent at home catering to our needs.

In my lifetime, I have never witnessed anyone who worked as hard or as long as our mother and never once did she complain or ask for anything in return.

When she served us our meals, she would sit silently smiling and watching as we gorged our small bellies. Afterwards, she would take all of our scraps and place them on a plate for her own meal to eat.

Most week nights our mother worked until eleven-thirty. My two oldest brothers, Jr. and Tootie, who otherwise should have been asleep, would have to stay awake in order to pick her up at the bus stop to walk her safely to our apartment after having worked a hard night's work.

This is the same woman, through my addiction I grew to shame and disrespect!

As I was maturing, I was a tiny child with a chip on my shoulder. I was much smaller and lighter than kids my own age. This made me feel self-conscious as I noticed that society seemed to favor the larger children. This inadequacy presented many problems which I sometimes face today, such as getting picked for basketball teams.

"Yeah, pick the big dummy, who's slow and can't make a hoop!"

Some people say that I suffer with what they call the "Napoleon" complex. I wanted to feel comfortable in my own skin, but it's those people who think they could take advantage of my small frame and easy going demeanor who create the problems.

Then they learn what I am truly capable of doing, usually the hard way. I found that I always have to prove my worth. Being raised in those projects, during heightened moments of the civil rights era and race riots also proved to be traumatic on my young soul. Those times were confusing.

Attending grade school I was being taught to love thy neighbor and to share, but outside that forum there was violence all around me. There were people starving and dying in front of my young eyes. It is a blessing that I survived through it all because we resided on a peninsula, completely blocked in...the only way in was the only way out! It was a mostly black community surrounded by South Boston, an all-white community whose racial antipathy was displayed with rock and bottle throwing each day as we made our way to work or school.

Back then, I had two good white friends that I met in school, but outside of school their parents forbid us to play together. We defied those orders by sneaking off to meet at pre-arranged destinations, usually somewhere peaceful and safe where we could enjoy each other's company. The racial hatred that was aimed at me, as well as the racial hatred that the blacks were aiming at the whites, caused me to feel fearful and psychologically inferior in my own brown skin.

It was during that period heroin was introduced into our community. It was as if a superior force had injected our neighborhood with megatons of that white powdery substance.

I found myself having to step over junkies who resembled sub-human-like creatures, scratching and nodding off in the drug paraphernalia littered project hallways. Most of the time, I was unable to tell if they were dead or alive.

Life in the Columbia Point projects was treacherous. Domestic abuse and rape were very prevalent. Men and women were often committing suicide by leaping off the high rise roofs or out of the yellow-brick seven story high windows. Back then I falsely believed that an exciting day for me consisted of my being able to sneak a climb on a fire truck or police car that careened through daily. We were poor and used these emergency vehicles much like carnival rides.

My siblings and I were also prideful as Mother rejected any government food assistance. Instead my brothers would walk me to the Stop and Shop mall where they'd stuff my pockets with food items then have me meet them outside.

I also falsely believed that these were exciting moments I enjoyed when an eighteen year old woman sexually seduced me. She taught me how to French-kiss and allowed me to squeeze and suck her breasts. Other times she coached me on how to place my tiny fingers into her hairy, moist vagina. Those same methods I also employed on girls of my own age. Today, I am convinced that those early actions contributed to programming my criminal thinking and compulsive behaviors.

By the time I reached the age of six years old, our mother had managed to climb the social ladder. After graduating college, she was selected for a prestigious position as an administrator director for a large health agency located in the Roxbury section of Boston. Earning higher wages she was then able to save enough money to move us out of these unhealthy, dangerous projects and into a three bedroom apartment located in the Mattapan section of Boston. At that time, Mattapan was a nice suburban neighborhood populated with a mixture of whites and blacks. Today it is mostly populated with blacks and is disgracefully known as "Murderpan" because of its drug and gang activity.

Our mother's new work schedule, pay increase and geographical change permitted her more time to drink and party with her friends. It wasn't long before she became increasingly violent towards my siblings and me. We all knew that the alcohol was the main contributor for her violent outbursts. When our mother wasn't drinking, she was the most caring and nurturing mother a child could ask for, but when she consumed alcohol - watch out!

Donald R. Frye

Over the course of only a short period of time she became so bad that we began hiding all belts and extension cords that she used to whip us with. Then she would become tired of searching the home for them and resorted to using her fists.

I'll never forget the time when our sister, Greta, stood up face-to-face with mom and tried to fight back. Our mother bobbed and weaved like an experienced prize fighter and flipped Greta over her back then smacked her up a few times. Meanwhile, she gave us the instant glare to convey the precise message that she is not to be challenged. Ever.

This incident is well etched in our minds and sometimes we look back on it and laugh. The boozing eventually began to take its toll on mother as she began showing signs of fatigue. We all knew that the alcohol was the culprit, but she continued to drink anyway. My siblings and I were stuck with the difficult decisions. We had to stand by and watch our mother waste away or try to help her.

Our way of helping her was by hiding her booze the same way we hid the belts and extension cords, but we quickly learned that this could become a tragic mistake on our part. After searching the entire apartment in an alcoholic rage, mother would grab the closest one of us to her and threaten to do him or her bodily harm if someone didn't hand over her booze.

One day we all got together and stood our ground against our mother and that became her turning point. Our stand along with the fact that she had developed high blood pressure was the moment she reached her bottom.

The doctors had warned her that if she continued to drink in that fashion she was going to die a premature death. To this day, I strongly believe that if she didn't love us or have us to care for her, she would have kept on drinking. When it came to her children, our mother refused to die and leave us all alone in this world unprotected. Our mother quit drinking and later became a successful black woman owning two properties.

During this difficult course of those times, our father resided across town in the Jamaica Plain section of Boston. It was a clean and quiet urban area. He always kept steadily employed and mailed our mother the court ordered financial support she needed to help care for us. I often wondered what our father would have done if there was no standing court order. He didn't present himself as the physical or conversational type of father outside of the swimming pool. I don't remember his ever checking my school progress reports or give me any positive reinforcements on my passing grades.

Although he was my swimming coach, he was never around to teach me social skills which I believed a child should learn from their father. For example, how to treat and respect women. The lack of his presence in my life outside of the swimming pool caused me to feel unwanted and resentful towards authoritative figures.

Occasionally he would stop by our home and bring gifts for me on my birthday. But often his presence seemed frigid. Even though I believe he loved me, I would have felt more secure if he would have taken the time to sit me down and look me in the eye and tell me those three words. I wanted him to simply hold me close as to re-assure me that his love was genuine. My father never provided me the protection I needed against my older siblings or society. Again, his actions caused me to feel vulnerable, fearful, or a burden to him.

Throughout the years, I never learned much about the type of man he is, but I continue to love him because he is my father.

I grew up wishing that there could be more to our relationship other than being

able to say "That's my coach. He's a great athlete!" I remember a time when I prank called and harassed his woman friend because I thought she was the one keeping him from me. It is one thing for a child to never have known who their father is, but to have one like I did, who didn't show enough love and affection, had a traumatic impact on my young soul. Throughout the years, I remained in contact with him hoping that we could build a relationship. That was wishful thinking. We were total strangers. The man in my life who I was supposed to look to for security was seldom there.

This is the man, whom with the aid of my addiction, I grew to shame and disrespect.

Donald R. Frye

Chapter

Two

CHOICES

Beginning at the age of six, I frequented the Roxbury Boys and Girls Club. It was a positive decision for at the time being there kept me busy after school and safe from the violent, treacherous streets. Throughout the years, I excelled in a variety of sports programs and helped to win quite a few swimming and diving championships.

My family moved again. We moved to a smaller and less expensive apartment with only two bedrooms. Our new home was located on Goodale Road in Mattapan, only a few streets away from our old place.

Our brother Tootie, who worked as a waiter at Fantasia Restaurant, had to sleep on the living room couch. Our sister Greta's bed was in the dining room where she decorated her walls with hundreds of Jackson Five posters. Her obsession with the singing group later motivated her to publish three novels titled *Obsessions, The Man in the Woods*, and the popular *Remember the Time*. In her novels, she reveals herself to be the real Billie Jean in Michael Jackson's life.

God rest his soul.

Our mother, of course, occupied the master bedroom which is also where our Shepherd/Collie mixed dog, Wendy, made herself comfortable under mom's bed, safe from us young children. I shared a tiny room with my oldest brother, Jr., and Rusty. To this day, I cannot fathom how we fit three beds in such a small space.

We also shared the broken drawers of a dark brown tattered dresser. My hamster, Joey, sitting on that dresser, constantly irritated me by gnawing and rattling the bars of his cage, trying to break free. I didn't know at that time that someday I would be sharing the same fate. One summer day, I released him into our back yard and wished him a better life.

My oldest brother, Jr. who is eight years older than I, occupied the bed nearest the window. When he made us angry, we used to tease him by calling him an African Bush-Boogie because he was a much darker complexion than the rest of us. He also had a large mole on the side of his nose, which he later had removed. Jr. was an intelligent, handsome young man.

He had many female and male friends who came to visit and stay the night.

One of his male friends took a real interest in me and after earning my trust, he would pull his penis out and fit it into my tiny hands. He would then instruct me on how to stroke it. At this developing stage of my life, other than my brothers, I had never seen a grown man's penis all covered with hair.

Although it felt wrong, fear and curiosity allowed me to play along. This man's penis felt huge in my small hands. I did not understand what was happening, but after a while, a white creamy substance flowed out of the tip, at which time he would withdraw my hands then wipe his penis on a piece of toilet paper. He would threaten me to not tell anyone. This sexual experience was unlike the experiences that I had with young women. I was not turned on by it. I was completely confused.

Also during this stage of my development, the Federal order for state wide busing was in full effect. The United

States National Guard and State Troopers had made their presence outside Boston Public Schools.

They were lined up in intimidating large numbers wearing dark colored riot gear. They carried loaded rifles, water cannons, batons and stood with trained police guard dogs. At such a young age these scenes were having a traumatic impact on my mental psyche.

Every day, instead of attending school to get an education, I sat in class shivering in fear for my life. Sometimes the authorities that were hired to protect me turned out to be the ones I needed to be protected from. There were constant protests and things often got out of control. The authorities would shoot us with water cannons and unleash the police dogs on the crowd.

I truly dreaded attending school so I played hooky as often as I could without being detected. Even with a poor attendance record, I managed to maintain a C-minus grade average, which in that era, was still sufficient enough for me to be promoted to the next grade level. Mother was pleased.

From the age of ten to fourteen, I mainly sheltered myself in the sports arena where I took a particular interest in aquatic sports. I enjoyed everything about being in the swimming pool and often imagined myself living there under water away from all of the disparity in the world. I would take a deep breath, hold it, and then swim under water in my very own fantasy world where things were much more peaceful.

Alas, eventually I would run out of air and have to surface and face the harsh reality of the world. I also had dreams and aspirations of becoming an oceanographer. The fiscal crisis at school and at home had a negative effect on my choices, causing me to dismiss it as highly improbable.

By the time I reached the age of fourteen, the mayor of the City of Boston had pulled the plug on most city funded sports and education programs. I was very traumatized by this decision and actions of wealthy people holding office. To me it appeared they no longer wanted to invest in our education, but instead in our incarceration. My parents were unable to afford the expenses for me to attend those programs, so with all this new time on my hands I began hanging out with the negative crowds.

In the beginning, I felt like a fish out of water trying to survive in a world that was not tailored to me. Kids my age were already smoking cigarettes, smoking marijuana, and drinking alcohol.

In the seventies, this appeared to be the culturally hip thing to do. African-Americans were mostly being portrayed in movies like Return of the Mack, Super Fly, Shaft, and Lady Sings the Blues. I began to emulate those characters. In the ninth grade I began drinking beer and smoking with the rest of the kids my age or older.

I falsely believed that drinking and getting high felt good and boosted my self-esteem. It provided me with the same euphoric feeling of escape that I experienced when swimming under water.

It helped me to suppress and evade my true and confused feelings and insecurities about my own character and what I witnessed occurring in my environment.

Getting high lent me the false courage I thought I needed to convince myself that I was invincible and mighty enough to survive in the most dangerous parts of the city.

At this early stage of my addiction, I was living a myth and began venturing deeper into the drug game and street life. Within a few weeks, I had uncovered the locations of the city's most infamous hot spots for kids my age. Every day, I drank alcohol and got high smoking weed. But weekends were special and more deserving of harder drugs.

On Fridays, I would cop some purple mescaline and powdered cocaine and would frequent an all-night house party over on Calendar Street in Dorchester. Sometimes gun play would ensue but I didn't worry about those dangers.

I would get completely stoned, dance and have unprotected sex with multiple female partners, sometimes right there on the dance floor. There were moments when I would over drink and had to kneel down on my knees in puddles of urine and place my face and hands on soiled toilets that were used by everyone throughout the night just to vomit.

I was living an extremely dangerous and self-destructive lifestyle but falsely believed that this lifestyle was normal activity for a kid my age.

Eventually, I began to build a larger tolerance for alcohol and drugs, so I needed more to keep me high. I began to do what was taught to me at a young age - steal and sell drugs in order to support my own addictions.

Playing the role of the drug dealer, I found had many perks. Perks such as getting high for free, women clinging to me like magnets, the money, and I was always dressed to impress. I believed that street hustlers had it made. It wasn't very long before I was introduced to the pimping game by a sexy yellow boned woman. Her stage name … **Peaches**.

Peaches was a few years older than me and turned me on to the downtown life. Peaches worked as a nude dancer and prostitute. She taught me many tricks of her trade. She was employed at the Naked Eye Strip Club located in the red-light district of downtown Boston. At the time, I was only a sixteen year old teenager, not even old

enough to enter the establishment where she worked. Yet Peaches somehow worked things out with the manager and not only was I allowed in, but was also served drinks just like any ordinary patron.

We usually hung out at the club until the end of her shift at two in the morning.

Afterwards, if she did not have any Johns to service, we would go cop some drugs if I didn't have any and head over to her apartment for an all-night sex, alcohol and drug orgy. My sexual experiences with Peaches caused me to contract a venereal disease for which I had to seek medical treatment.

Throughout these developing stages, I was able to charm my school teachers and maintain a C-minus grade average through my high school years. But when I entered the twelfth grade, my life had spiraled out of control.

I was still in absolute denial. I had yet to realize the effect drugs and alcohol were having on me.

I was making money pimping and selling drugs. That's all that mattered to me. I dropped out of high school in the first quarter of the twelfth grade but hurried and obtained my high school equivalency diploma. I did this to satisfy my mother who at that time was my biggest enabler.

An enabler is a person who unwittingly supports an addict's habit.

My mother, God rest her soul, was very protective of me, but also naive about the drug game and street life. I was able to easily manipulate her into believing my made up stories and get her to unsuspectingly finance my alcohol and drug ventures.

Before quitting high school, I had met and be-friended a young lady named Rhonda, who was intelligent and extremely attractive female. She compares to the classy elegance and beauty of the young actress, Lisa Ray. Her inviting stares are what made her special to me. Unlike the other girls that came before her, she had me mesmerized into seeing our unborn children. Rhonda possessed the sort of inner and outer beauty that could make any frugal outfit look expensively designed. These days she would be labeled as a dime. She also possessed an innocence that I craved and would not be in denial.

From the moment I first laid my eyes on her, I felt spiritually connected to her and wanted to spend the rest of my life in her company. Up until this moment, no woman had this effect on me. We started dating regularly and discovered that we had a few things in common. We discovered it was mainly the spiritual chemistry that we shared. It connected us and allowed our joint souls to evolve into a well-orchestrated symphony of true love. When we first met, she confessed to being a virgin. I respected her enough to allow her the space and time to grow familiar and comfortable with me.

During our long courtship, I would visit her every day after work and sit with her on the living room sofa for hours admiring her awesome, untainted beauty. I had still been seeing other girls, but only for the purposes of extracting money from them to support my drug habits. Over time Rhonda became my new obsession. She became someone I depended on to shelter me from the cruel world. For a while, I even toned down my criminal activities and began seeking entry into college or a trade school. I kept employed as a lifeguard at the Fairlawn Estates swimming pool. I continued drinking, but falsely believed that everything in my life was in order and that I was in control.

I lived in a state of denial.

When Rhonda finally caved into my subtle demands for sex we were in bliss. Three months later she announced she was pregnant. This news was a wonderful, yet unexpected surprise that sparked some controversial differences within our relationship. Although I wanted her to have my children, I still blamed her for not having used protection. The fact of the matter was that we were both equally responsible for our inactions. Neither one of us was experienced enough to have a child, we were still young and uneducated. I fell in love with this extremely attractive young woman who seemed all men wanted to seduce. Rhonda could have the pick of the litter and she chose me. My constant use of alcohol and drugs caused me to start feeling self-conscious about myself and our relationship.

I began to obsess over my insecure feelings, but I never discussed my feelings with her because my pride would not let me. Instead, I began tearing her down to my

level of ignorance by calling her names like stupid and dummy. I began treating Rhonda like an instrument. To me she was no longer an expecting mother, someone's daughter, sister, or cousin. Instead, Rhonda was mine. I was not going to share her with the rest of the world. She was not permitted out of the house without me unless she was on a short leash of an approved relative or friend. Soon

I became envious and more verbally abusive to her and on many occasions while under the influence of alcohol or drugs I placed our lives in danger.

One such occasion occurred after we gave birth to our baby girl, Elizabeth, whom we named after my mother. It was on Rhonda's birthday and rather than spend it with her, I was out getting high with two other girls. At one point in the evening, I blanked out and decided to return home to pack some of our belongings. My intoxicated and drugged state of mind led me into moving our small family to New York City at four o'clock that morning.

After I packed our things into my green 1973 Chrysler Newport Custom and with only one-quarter tank of gas and fourteen cents in my pocket, we hit the road for the Big Apple. I don't know what the heck I was thinking because I didn't even know anyone who even lived in New York City!

Still, I had our baby girl lying on the back seat of the car wrapped in a stolen mink coat. She was oblivious to the dangers that her own father was subjecting her to. As we were passing through Rhode Island, we had a minor fender bender. The car was still operating sufficiently enough for me to continue on with the journey. Further down the road to New York City, the car broke down on the interstate highway bordering Connecticut, so we spent the early morning hours stuck in the break down lane of a four lane highway as it started pouring rain.

Not only was this a dangerous place to be parked, but Rhonda started to fuss about our child being hungry for some milk. In a rush to get us some help, I decided to leave them there alone on that dangerous highway. I climbed a fence then cautiously slid down the wet grassy embankment of the road and entered a neighborhood of one-family homes. I knocked on the front door of the first house I came to expecting to get us some help. When no one answered the door, I broke into the house and took the liberty to pack some of these stranger's belongings and actually fix us some sandwiches as if there was nothing wrong with what I was doing.

Afterwards, I casually walked back to the car where Rhonda and baby Elizabeth sat waiting for me to return. I never knew what could possibly have been going on in Rhonda's mind at that moment, but I did not care. About one half-hour later, I decided to cross the highway median, dodging all traffic where I again descended the embankment. I broke into the first house I came to with no one home. This time when I broke the window pane, an alarm was triggered and instead of taking off, I boldly climbed on the roof of the home and disengaged the alarm by snatching the wires loose. I then entered the home and packed a suitcase full of valuable items and walked casually across the highway back to the car without a care or worry in the world. It was by the grace of God that we never made it to the Big Apple. Who knows what sort of dangers I would have placed us in.

Later that morning, a Good Samaritan showed up and helped me get my car running. I drove us back to Boston where I ended this terrible journey by slamming my car into the thick oak tree that stood in front of my mother's home. After a few days of rest, I went out and traded my stolen treasures for drugs and cash to buy some booze.

Rhonda was now co-dependent. Regardless of my negative lifestyle and aggressions towards her, she would always make up excuses for me in order to keep our small family together. She still sensed some good qualities in me and believed in me and in us. I promised her that I would keep our small family together. I promised her that I would leave the streets, booze, and drugs in exchange for her hand in marriage.

Consequential

GG
Stone 09

Chapter

Three

CONSEQUENCES

Prior to exchanging our vows, I continued making bad choices and acting on impulse. I landed in Massachusetts Probate Court challenging a paternity suit. I was eventually exonerated, but nevertheless was exposed for my infidelities. The young lady who purportedly claimed me as her baby's father was very resentful at my denial and request for a blood test. Even though the results were negative, she still conjured up some lies that got the Glenway Street Gang to kill me.

After several attempts on my life, I decided to get away by joining the United States Army Reserves as a private in Fort Jackson, South Carolina. Even there I continued to drink with my new Army buddies.

After returning home from six weeks of basic training, I discovered that not much had changed on those vicious streets of Boston. I decided to escape the wrath of those street gangs by joining the regular Army on a full-time basis.

Donald R. Frye

Rhonda and I were married on November 6, 1982. Soon after, I was deployed to Fort Hood, Texas. It houses the largest armored tank battalion in the United States. Our plan was for me to arrive at the base ahead of them and set up the living arrangements for Rhonda and the baby.

I allowed my addiction to get in the way of that as well. All I did was rationalize the situation by thinking that things would only get better once my family arrives. I selfishly spent most of our money partying on the new scene that there was barely enough money left over from my paycheck for me to complete the travel and living arrangements for my wife and daughter. I was compelled to take on a two-month pay advance and a two-hundred dollar bank overdraft which placed us in deep debt even before we got started.

I rented us a small, cozy looking cottage apartment outside the gates of the Army base in the city of Killeen. The three of us got settled in. In the beginning, I couldn't afford a vehicle and there was no public transportation. Every day I had to hitch a ride to and from work. The low wages I was earning being a private kept our budget extremely tight, but each day I still managed to feed my addiction. In order for me to support my addiction, sometime I would go to the supermarket and steal our food and other cosmetic items that we needed each day.

The more I stole, the more I got high, and the more bad choices I would make. My compulsive behaviors were being amplified by the consumption of alcohol and drugs. The more bad choices that I made, the more likely I was forced to make my wife appear more dumb than me. The more abusive I became, the more I hated myself. We were caught up in a very dangerous and vicious cycle that caused me to feel fearful, insecure, and paranoid. At this stage, I realized that I had a problem, but I would rationalize the situation by convincing myself that drinking and using drugs was the cultural and social thing to do. Everybody does it. I could stop anytime I wanted to.

Looking back at myself at the young age of twenty, I am convinced that is when I began to suffer from drug psychosis.

Generally, I was experiencing psychotic behaviors that were being induced by the consumption of alcohol and drugs. Back then, I did not recognize the symptoms. To me, everything was normal because all my faculties were intact. This vicious cycle continued and to support my increasing urges which now consisted of such west-coast entrees as crystal meth, blotter acid, and purple haze, I began pawning our household gadgets and lifting more things from the stores. The more I stole, the more drunk and high I was able to get. The more I continued to use, the more I became filled with self-hatred. I grew fearful and insecure about my marriage. The more insecure I became, the more I had to push my wife down to my level of ignorance so that she wouldn't leave me.

I continued calling her names like cream puff, softy, and dummy. In reality, I was taking my own insecurities out on my again pregnant wife and was speaking about myself when calling her those names. Over time, I became a full-fledged coward and began psychologically and physically abusing my wife. I would yell and twist her arms in front of our baby girl Elizabeth. Elizabeth was three years old and had a sibling on the way.

Elizabeth and I had a very strong bond from the day she was born and her tiny body was placed in my arms. It was as if the umbilical cord was now attached to me. She was daddy's little girl, and I was her hero and protector. But later, with the aid of my addiction, I severed that tight bond. I was only eighteen when she was born. I was naïve as to how to care for a newborn child. Elizabeth did not come with any instructions and my addiction would not allow me to take the time to purchase any baby care literature much less do any extensive research on how to raise a child.

Instead, I acted irresponsibly and relied upon the mythical knowledge that was conveyed to me by other drunks and addicts who like myself, could not tell day from night.

Now with a new sibling on the way for Elizabeth to grow up with, Rhonda and I were somehow still in great spirits. Some of our loans were paid off and we were becoming adjusted to the Army life. We had moved closer to the Army base to get out of the rodent infested trailer we had moved into. The new location proved to be worse, and much more stressful on us.

We had rented a forty-foot beige and white trailer that sat in a congested trailer park. It at first sight appeared adequate for us. The first winter, the entire trailer got flooded from a busted pipe. The heating and ventilation systems, we discovered, were not even attached to the inside of the trailer! We were wasting hard earned money that I could have used to get high and was heating the outside! We had to purchase electric heaters to keep warm. That cost also cut down on my addiction expenses, making me angry.

This problem had increased our electricity bill three-fold. I made verbal complaints to the management of the trailer park who acted nonchalantly about our situation. Meanwhile, we were living in complete squalor with a young child and expectant mother. I was fuming and felt that I needed to hold the manager accountable for endangering our lives. Our complaints seem to fall on deaf ears. That is until I filed a written complaint with the military officials who became involved in the matter. An investigator was sent to our home at which time we were promised by the housing authority of the trailer park that things would get fixed right away.

By then, things had become worse so I was expecting for us to be moved into a hotel at their expense until the task was completed. But that isn't what transpired. We were given plastic tarp to cover our wet floors while we waited another two weeks until the carpenters arrived to fix the problem. I grew angry at the cowardly manner in which I believed I handled the situation. I became obsessed with the thoughts of how I could have done more to protect my family. As usual, I went and got drunk and high. I blamed Rhonda for suggesting that we move to this trailer in the first place.

After nine months of pregnancy, our second child entered this world at Darnell Army Hospital. She was such a beautiful child. We named her Gertrude. We called her Trudy for short, after my wife's mother. Trudy brought new meaning and hope to our home. But the added expense of a newborn quickly infringed upon financing my drinking and getting high. So, in order for me to maintain my status quo, I began stealing cases of Similac milk, diapers, baby lotions and soaps. All the fixings needed to keep a new born baby clean and happy.

Our daughter Trudy was maybe two months old when my wife requested that we purchase our baby girl some new clothes.

Donald R. Frye

My response to her request, "What two-month old baby needs clothes? She doesn't do anything or go anywhere!"

To me all our baby girl did was sleep, eat and shit. I told my wife that our baby was just fine wearing a long bed-shirt given to her at the hospital. After some coaxing from my wife, I finally drove us to the mall and instructed Rhonda to pick out some outfits for both our girls. When the carriage was full with the things we needed, I took those items and stuffed them into a shopping bag that I had concealed in my Army fatigues. Afterwards, I passed the bag to my wife and escorted her out of the department store with both of our children in tow. Therefore, Trudy's first set of clothes were stolen and the money we saved went towards my getting drunk and high.

In fact, everything at this stage of my addiction was primarily focused on staying drunk and high. I began stealing scrap metal from my job and selling small amounts of drugs. I brought a gun to do stick ups. I was also cruising the red-light district of downtown Killen searching for my own prostitutes to pimp.

I was totally out of control and deeply mired back into the unpredictable street life again.

I grew disgusted in myself. I felt morally and spiritually bankrupt.

I wanted to end my life. Every day I drove to work contemplating smashing my car head on into the huge concrete pillars that supported the highway overpass. My wife became extremely fearful of me. Things at home changed for Rhonda went from worse to terrible to intolerable. For the first time ever, I open-handedly smacked my wife, bruising her pretty golden face. She responded by informing the military authorities of my violent behaviors towards her and they removed me from our home.

After a short inquiry, I admitted to being wrong. I was then ordered to participate in a twelve week cycle of a men's group who battered their spouses. I was also ordered to attend only two AA meetings and watch a film on addiction. This experience was to have been my first introduction to AA/NA but I easily managed to skip out of them undetected.

At this stage, I honestly believed I didn't need any help to get my life back on track.

I also tried to skip out on the men's group, but they were very strict on attendance. The men's group syllabus consisted of us watching films with mock cases of spousal abuse followed by discussion. Most times I smoked a joint before the session, and sat there through the two hour session without speaking a word. I hardly paid any attention to what the other men had to share.

At home things were business as usual. I continued to drink and do drugs. The vicious cycle kept revolving and playing itself through.

In 1984, I got busted for selling marijuana and cocaine to an undercover military intelligence officer. Our orders to transfer overseas to Germany were flagged. I was now faced with two felony charges and the end of my Army career. I had really screwed up this time and knew I was headed toward doing time at the Fort Leavenworth Federal Prison in Kansas.

Before going to court to answer for those charges, I had moved my wife and children back home to Boston, Massachusetts, where they stayed with relatives until finding a place of their own. I continued to work but now lived on base quarters. Any money that I did not send home to support my family, went towards booze and drugs. I no longer cared because I was going to prison.

"So what the heck," I thought.

I began spending my nights partying at a night club called the Rising Sun whose moniker was staying open until eight in the morning. I used to store my work uniforms in my car and leave the club to work drunk and high. This presented many dangers because I was trained as a heavy equipment mechanic and operator. I handled up to sixty-ton vehicles on a daily basis.

One evening, I got so stinking drunk that I started dancing with a stranger who at first glance appeared to be a nice looking red-bone chick. We bumped, grinded and kissed through several songs. Afterwards, she brought me to her apartment so we could have sex. That is when I discovered that she was a transvestite. I was so stoned and drunk that after the initial shock wore off, I decided, "what-the-heck," and had unprotected sex with this *girl*. I had stooped to an all-time low. I felt there is no act, violent or otherwise, that I wouldn't perform before heading off to prison.

I continued to get obliterated. The higher I got, the more fearful I became about serving time in federal prison. I had gotten into so much more trouble that I was confined to the base by my commanding officer. The thought of going off to prison and not seeing my wife and daughters plagued my every obsessive thought. One day, I left the base and went AWOL (Absent Without Leave). I returned to Boston by airplane and winded up putting my mother through torture worrying about the dangers that I posed.

I pulled sneaky stunts on people for drugs and in retaliation for my thievery, the front windows to my mother's house were broken out. My oldest brother, fearing my mother's safety, ended up having to turn me in to the authorities. I was extradited back to Texas where I had to answer the criminal charges plus an added charge for going AWOL.

I went to trial and was sentenced to eighteen months hard labor at the United States Army Correctional Activity (USACA) in Kansas. The entire time there I managed to stay high. I often called home to check to make sure that my wife was in the house. While in prison, I had the opportunity to attend AA/NA groups and meetings and earn time off my sentence. I also could have earned time off my sentence for my participation in other recovery groups as well.

Yet, I remained in complete denial, and used to make fun of the men and women who attended those programs. For me to attend sober programs was a sign of weakness.

I was not weak, not l'il 'ole me!

After serving my time in prison, I returned home with a lump sum of money that I had saved up. I was welcomed by my wife and two beautiful daughters. They were about three and six years old. They saw no beneficial change in my attitude.

If anything, I had become worse.

First, I accused my wife of being unfaithful while I was away in prison. Then

I spent all our money on alcohol and drugs. What few things I did purchase for our home, I eventually brought back to the store or sold. I returned items such as our floor model color television, stereo, and even my wife's wedding ring.

Pawning her ring was the straw that broke the camel's back. My wife ordered me to immediately move out of the house. She claimed that I was endangering her and our children by using and selling drugs out of our home. I also spent our daughters' money out of their piggy banks. Things became drastically worse because I feared getting kicked out. I introduced my wife to crack cocaine thinking she would let me stay. That evening, Rhonda warned me after taking one hit of the crack pipe, *"It feels too good Donald."*

But I just kept feeding it to her hoping she would let me stay.

My wife finally staged an all-out protest to my negative lifestyle that was endangering our family. It sparked enough rage in me to knock her to the floor in front of our daughters. I kicked her in the head with my Nike sneaker like a football player kicking a field goal. Our oldest daughter, Elizabeth, screamed at me to stop. She then ran to the telephone. I followed her in hot pursuit. I snatched the phone away from her tiny hands and slammed the receiver back into its cradle, cracking the side. Then I smacked any love my child had left for me at that time out of her face. Afterwards, I departed the scene and was never again allowed back home.

I was also kicked out of my mother's house. She had grown suspicious and afraid of me because I had stolen from her. For days, I roamed the dangerous streets of Boston stalking my prey. I began scamming anyone who was foolish enough to trust me with their money or drugs. Eventually, there wasn't a street I could walk down without fear of running into someone seeking deadly retribution for the slick stunts that I had pulled on them. Unknowingly, anyone who hung around me was in danger of being hurt or killed. The ironic truth of the matter was that I really wasn't concerned with dying or being harmed. My main concern was with how difficult it was to fuel my addiction under such extreme and dangerous circumstances.

I could not continue to live this way. I was exhausted from sneaking around and hiding in the shadows. I fled to Syracuse, New York.

Chapter

Four

VICIOUS CYCLE

In early summer 1987, I arrived in Syracuse, New York where I stayed with my second oldest brother, Tootie. He had been eagerly expecting me. I was not there for any geographical cure, but only to find somewhere safe to feed my addiction in peace, not having to peek over my shoulder every minute.

Tootie resided in the East Fayette Street Apartments, which were basically subsidized projects that were much cleaner than the bricks in Boston. They looked more like real apartments. The elevators in the building actually worked!

When I arrived, my brother gladly welcomed me with open arms. With pride he introduced me to his neighbors and friends. It was obvious to me that no one in our family had warned him of the possible dangers that I possessed. Besides being brothers, we had another thing in common. We both drank alcohol. It had been many years since I had seen my brother. Years before, he up and moved to Syracuse with his girlfriend. But, before leaving, they both had stayed at our mother's house in Boston. I was sixteen at that time and used to sell weed with him.

For the first three days in Syracuse, my brother and I drank beer, listened to music and reminisced about the past. We got caught up on the who's who and doing what in the family. During the day, Tootie worked at a child care facility as a counselor. My plans were to seek employment, and save enough cash to move out on my own.

The first day I left the apartment to go job hunting, I wound up breaking into a house and robbed strangers of their possessions. I sold and traded my newly found treasures for drugs and cash for alcohol. By the time my brother arrived home from work, I was drunk and high as a hot air balloon floating alone in the stratosphere. There was plenty more for him to join in on the festivities. I never told him where I got the money in which to finance this party and he never once asked.

The treasures from my heist fueled my addiction for several days. I actually netted enough for a security deposit and one month's rent in my own place, but my mind was only programmed towards staying high. When the money finally ran out, it was time for me to go seek employment again. This time I carried my brother's gun with me. He kept a chrome plated forty-five under his mattress for protection. I borrowed it to do a stick up which I had previously cased out at a gas station over on the south side of town. It was early in the morning, so after forcing the cashier to give me the money, I made away with only a couple of hundred dollars, probably the cash drawer to start the work day. It was still enough to fuel my addiction.

When my brother arrived home, there was a condescending look on his face as he entered into the drinking and rouging festivities I had set up for us. When I told him about the heist, he had a look of concern on his face. I thought that he'd understand since robbery was his past forte.

Instead, he acted very apprehensive toward my actions. Later that week, I showed up at my brother's apartment with some street thugs whom I met at the corner and he kicked us out. When I showed up alone, he let me in to eat and sleep. That very next morning after Tootie left for work, I woke up and packed my things along with a few of his fine two-piece suits that were stored in his closet, in protective plastic bags. I secured his pistol in my waistband and locked the door behind me. I stepped over to my brother's next door neighbor's apartment and left them his keys to the apartment. I had no plans on coming back there anytime soon.

Afterwards, I made my way into the mean sections of Syracuse. I proceeded to a neighborhood bar where I sold my brother's suits. I then went and located a drug den and sat down and got high. When I ran out of money, I sold my brother's gun. I was never really a gun person and carrying one on me while I was high always made me paranoid and fearful of being sent to jail for a strict mandatory minimum sentence.

It was early evening when I tapped out of money and I hadn't eaten all day. My pockets were empty and my body was fatigued. I needed help but detox never once entered my thoughts. I roamed around the streets in a stupor for a couple of hours before entering good 'ol Charlie's Night Club, which was located in the vicinity of Syracuse University. The club was a student hangout and I made it in just before the cover charge began. I strolled around the club and quickly made friends with some reveling students, who to my benefit, sat in a booth with a table completely covered with pitchers of beer and food.

Later that evening, I met a young woman who I confided in. After hearing my made up stories, she booked us into a motel room for the night. I discovered that she worked as an accountant for the Archdioceses. She was an innocent young woman named Karen who sometimes frequented the wild side. Knowing this information, it only took me a couple of days to manipulate her into embezzling money she counted at work so we could smoke cocaine. She became the slave to both me and the cocaine.

It wasn't long before she was prostituting for me. Within three months she was burnt out and appeared to have reached her bottom. She had lost her job and the respect of most of her family and friends who forced her into detox and rehab. Karen's absence left me hurting for cash. Over this period, I had grown very dependent on her for everything and had mentally lost my will to survive alone.

After her departure, I still had two pre-paid days left on my motel room, so I used this time to get completely obliterated. At times, I sat in that small, lonely motel room drunk and wondering how I got this way.

Finally, I admitted defeat and fell to my knees and asked God help.

I prayed too for the well-being of my wife and children. I sobbed completely through the night. When I was all cried out and the bottles of booze were entirely empty, I left the motel room depressed and checked into the University Hospital Detox Center.

I was greeted at the receptionist desk by professional clinical staff who understood my needs. Without hesitation, they signed me into their ten-day in-patient detox program that required me to participate in daily discussion groups and attend AA/NA meetings. Within two days, my thoughts had become clearer. Before, everything was just a blur. My body was also growing healthier and stronger. This new feeling was enjoyable, so I eagerly contemplated committing myself into the extensive thirty-day recovery program.

During treatment, I listened intensely and also shared in the groups with women and men like me. I discovered that I was not alone in this dreadful vicious cycle.

The counseling staff was very professional and understanding, except on the fifth day when they dismissed me from the program because of my radical racial views. At that time, I was the only black person receiving treatment. Trying to discover the roots of my addiction, the group therapist had asked me why I believed I drank alcohol or did drugs. I tried to share truthfully with the group and expressed some subdued feelings I felt towards my social and economic background.

I also raised my concerns about the racial discrimination in which I had experienced. The subject sparked some controversial debates. Rather than allow us as a group to continue to collectively explore the subject which I was adamant about discussing, the counselor expelled me from the detox program against better judgment for my continuous need for treatment.

With only a few days rest and relaxation under my belt, I once again took to the streets. I went and hung around the University night posts where I met up with some street hustlers from Buffalo, New York. They had just arrived in town to attend a concert being held at the Carrier Dome, home of the Syracuse Orangemen. These hustling dudes seemed to have their game tight. They were operating as a team of bandits who traveled on concert tours selling swag or dummy (fake) drugs to unsuspecting customers. They took a liking to my street skills and allowed me to travel along with them. While traveling with them, I learned many tricks of the swag game and that first night, we got paid. We rented adjoining hotel rooms for partying with lots of real drugs, alcohol, and of course, some prostitutes. The very next day, the Buffalo boys, as I had started to call them, departed Syracuse via Greyhound Bus. They were heading to Rochester to re-up on supplies. They had invited me to join them, but I decided to stay in Syracuse.

Before leaving, they were generous enough to leave me enough alcohol and drugs to keep me going for a day and night. When those ran out, I went and slept in the drunk tank located at the downtown Syracuse Rescue Mission. After sleeping it off, I simply turned back into a lost soul, drinking and wandering through town all day. Sometimes I found myself sobbing while calling out to my wife and daughters whom I missed so much.

"Rhonda, Elizabeth, Trudy," I pleaded, "Please forgive me. I love you!"

I staggered past crowds of people who would glance at me sort of oddly, probably because I gave the appearance of a young homeless teenager. At the time, I was about twenty-five years old, but with my small boyish frame and face, I looked many years younger and could easily pass as a troubled teen.

Almost every night, without fail, at two or three o'clock in the morning, the rescue mission staff could count on my making an appearance with a high alcohol content reading. The staff kept urging me to sign into a program but I refused. I was still in denial about my addiction.

I was adamant I could quit on my own.

I continued going out everyday scamming people and getting drunk. At one point, I was hanging out at gay bars searching for easy victims to stick up. I once got arrested for prostitution. After leaving the county jail and then about twenty different nights of sleeping it off in the drunk tank, I finally admitted defeat and committed myself into the 30-day extended substance abuse program.

The staff at the rescue mission allowed me to detox for five days before transferring me over to the extended program located on the opposite side of the red-brick building. The co-ed living quarters were immaculate, the food appetizing, and the staff and other clients were very inviting. I participated in the substance abuse program for three weeks and during this time I had gained some weight and pigmentation had returned to my skin. I participated in groups by sharing some of my past experiences and future plans with women and men who were just like me. Lost and turned out, due to our addictions.

In that short period of sobriety, I discovered that life wasn't fair even when I wasn't drunk or high.

Our program group traveled on a couple of outings to the 300. We also attended a concert and those trips gave me the opportunity to explore the outdoors while being sober.

The sober experience felt wonderful. In only three weeks' time I learned good things that helped me understand more about addiction and what was going on with me.

I learned that a substance abuser is a person who abuses substance using a distinguished pattern, quantity, which often negatively affects one's lifestyle.

At this juncture, I believed that I was ready to live a manageable life. During my stay at the program, I constantly wondered about my beautiful wife and young daughters. How were they doing?

I prayed for their safety and well-being. I became depressed, and decided to leave the program to go find them. After conferring with them about leaving, the counselors urged me to stay for the duration of the treatment, but I departed against their sound advice. My cunning addiction led me to believe I was cured enough to make it on my own.

After acquiring enough money for a bus ticket to Boston, I headed home to be reunited with my family. But, not before stopping off at the liquor store to purchase myself a beer. I figured with almost one month clean and sober, I could resolve myself to just one drink. Still, I was in complete denial.

As soon as I took that first drink, the alcohol dragged me straight back to hell as if to punish me for neglecting it for so long. I ended up getting obliterated before traveling to Boston and embarrassingly discovered that my wife had moved with our two daughters to Minneapolis, Minnesota. I was hurt after finding them gone and I didn't have a clue as to where or how to get in touch with them. Somewhere deep in my conscience, I knew that they would be safer away from me as long as I continued to use.

I arrived at my mother's home looking and acting respectable enough for her to invite me in despite the wrong I had committed against her. I was her youngest child and knew that she would never deny me. I stayed with her for a few days and even got the chance to speak on the phone with my daughters. My wife wouldn't divulge her new address out of fear I would show up at their door unannounced. Rhonda barely was able to talk with me out of fear that I would somehow smooth talk her into letting me come home to them. My wife was not aware that at this point of our lives, I wanted to be free from alcohol and drugs and live a normal married life with her and our children. However, my addiction continued to keep me in many states of denial.

Often times I would compare myself to others who I thought were in worse shape than I was. After hearing my daughter's voices over the telephone, I became depressed and felt a strong urge to drink and get high. This urge overcame me. I lacked any sober foundation or support system. Since my mother hadn't planned to cook, I asked her for a few bucks for a bite to eat at the neighborhood sub shop. I left the house only to join up with a few of my old hanging buddies on their way to cop some alcohol and drugs. I pitched in what I had and after just one hit off the crack pipe, I became very fearful and paranoid.

I couldn't help thinking about all those people still out there waiting to settle a score with me for robbing them, then skating out of town to Syracuse. By the time the drugs were out, my mind was racing and I began feenin for another hit to boost my confidence. I was afraid to get out and hustle on the streets. I had no idea who was after me or where they may be lurking. I crept back to my mother's house and sat around with her and waited for when she went to the bathroom. Then like a slimy snake, I slivered into her bedroom and stole some money out of her pocketbook. My mother was a landlord and she held a huge stack of money, probably the mortgage money, but I didn't care. I only took enough to get me off of empty which was about fifty bucks. When she returned to her seat on the sofa, I acted normal and waited a few moments to pass and then made a phony call within her ear shot. After hanging up the phone, I excused myself for the evening by lying to her, telling her that I was leaving to go visit a female friend. What she did not know was that my friend is crack cocaine, what we addicts refer to as the White Bitch - cocaine in its purest form.

Once outside, I slithered my way to Mattapan Square where I ran into my man, Globes. His name is short for snowball. A name I gave him because of his large head in proportion to his slender frame, plus his wide bright sneaky grin. Globes owned a two-tone brown and beige Ford Escort, which was parked nearby. He was on his way to cop some booze and crack. I joined him. It was coincidental that when I explained to him about how I came upon the money, he confessed to having just done the same thing. He stated that the tenants who rent the first-floor apartment at his mother's house handed him an envelope containing their month's rent. Globes was suppose to give this envelope to his mother which was what he usually did when she got home, but instead Globes slid the envelope under his mother's locked bedroom door. His mother always kept the room secure when she wasn't home for fear that he would steal from her again. Globes began feenin for a hit of crack cocaine, so he unraveled a clothes hanger then fished the envelope back out from under the door.

The only difference in our scams was that Globes had kept the entire contents of the envelope. Now we both faced the dire consequences of not being able to go home because we had stolen money from our mothers to support our addictions. We went and got drunk and high throughout most of that night, then passed out in the car.

The next morning, I hipped him to the way the Buffalo Boys made the fake stuff. We then proceeded to a grocery store where we stole some sweet basil and Elmer's glue. We made a fresh batch of the fake tie-stick weed. The both of us drove around all day tricking people then hurried off to feed our own addiction. We also did an occasional unarmed robbery if we ran into a potential easy victim. This run lasted for four months. Every day we broke the law to get the money we needed to feed our habits.

No one was exempt.

It all came to an abrupt end the day I totaled his car. That evening I had sniffed some heroin then nodded off at the wheel almost killing us and rendering his car useless. Without transportation we were doomed. It was too dangerous for us to walk the streets of Boston after having stolen from so many people. The only option I had to survive was to check into the volunteer prisoner detox program which was at the South East Correctional Facility in Bridgewater, Massachusetts.

In the past, there existed a voluntary detox program within the state prison system. When I entered, they placed me in the infirmary to treat my alcohol tremors with the drug Librium. Once I recovered from the shakes, I was placed in the general population and attended some well-established outside recovery groups, AA/NA meetings, and films. During my stay I also spoke to a counselor who gave me the option for further rehabilitation in another facility, such as a therapeutic program or halfway house. I declined all offers still thinking I would be able to handle this on my own.

I telephoned my mother from the prison to check how she was doing and to apologize for stealing her money. She seemed to be elated to hear my voice and to know that I was still alive somewhere. After all of the sneaky stunts I have pulled, she not only forgave me, but she also express mailed me thirty dollars for me to purchase incidentals.

During those ten days at the prison detox, I attend AA/NA meetings where I got a chance to hear some extremely disturbing testimonies from convicts who were there serving life sentences as a result of their addictions. At that time, I thought that these experiences could never happen to me.

I later found out those were called *"yets"*.

Many times the meetings were being used by the cons as a meeting place for them to pass contraband items then return back to their cells. This was a very serious situation but I still felt that this wasn't a very effective program for me. These feelings allowed my addiction to continue to plague my emotions. After the ten days were over, I departed the prison and immediately went and got drunk and high as if my life depended on it.

I repeated this same prison detox routine four times in just that one summer. Each time I went out things appeared to get worse because I began committing more brazen offenses and knew that it wouldn't be very long before I got sent to prison for real.

The only other thought I had was about how long. Finally, my desire to get sober landed me at High Point Academy in Plymouth, Massachusetts, near where the pilgrims supposedly had sailed in on the Mayflower and discovered America.

High Point was a thirty day intense substance abuse treatment program. I was welcomed into the groups and one-on-one therapy. The staff was very professional and amongst some of their established curriculum, I was instructed on the three stages of addiction:

-episodic

-habitual

-chronic

We also discussed family roles. In my case, it was determined that I played the role of the alcoholic and drug addicted husband and father. We discussed the effects of such other roles as co-dependent (wife), scapegoat (child), and introvert (child). All roles used to mask the troubles caused by the alcoholic father.

At the end of the treatment, we were taken to an AA Convention in Hyannis Port, Massachusetts. It was an awesome program filled with love and understanding. I truly felt as if I had accomplished something great. After completing the thirty-day program, I volunteered to be placed in a halfway house to continue my treatment. But the nearest available space had a waiting list several months long.

The caring staff at the program tried to get me placed in a holding program but they too were filled to capacity. With no other available option, I was then released to a wet homeless shelter with no support system to live amongst the active users. I couldn't go stay at my mother's house.

On my last visit home, I ducked the corner when I arrived to see my mother leaving the house. I wanted for her to walk down the street and turn the corner. When she was out of sight, I proceeded to climb through her living room window then hastily shook down the house for cash. When I didn't find any, I took her portable Sony Cassette player and left. Afterwards, I scurried around the block to visit the basketball court where all the young crack dealers hung out then presented the cassette player to one of them. The young man checked out the system before handing me a ten-dollar piece of crack in exchange. As I was hurrying away with thoughts of getting high on my mother's expense, the kid smashed the cassette player over my head announcing, "That's for taking your mother's radio!" as if reading my thoughts. I took off running for fear he would want the crack back.

That was before the High Point Program. Now after completing the program, I was forced back into the mean streets and I began using right away. Two weeks faded by with my ripping and running in and out of homeless shelters before I signed back into another rehab. This time, I checked into the Boston Detox Program located at the Lemmuel Shattuck Hospital, located in Jamaica Plain. After completing another detox, the staff placed me into a co-ed holding program within the hospital awaiting an extended program or hallway house.

During my stay at the hospital, I became physically acquainted with a female client. We were caught having unprotected sex. We were immediately dismissed from the program for failing to obey the rules. We were forbidden to have physical contact between staff or clients. After being kicked out of the program, I roamed the streets for a few days contemplating my next move. Finally, I phoned my mother who knew how desperate I had become and was trying to get clean and sober.

My mother agreed to pay the travel expenses for me to go stay with my oldest brother, Jr. and his family in San Diego, California.

HADES   by Shane '09'

Chapter

Five

HADES

After all the awful things that I put my dear mother through, she still continued to care enough to meet me downtown Boston at the Greyhound Bus Depot to see me off to San Diego, California. My mom used her credit card to charge a one-way bus ticket to California, then handed me some spending money to see me through my three and one-half day journey across the good ole USA. Since my bus had not arrived, this gave us some moments to spend together before my departure. I coaxed my mom to walk with me to a nearby store to purchase some reading material for the bus ride. I knew darn well that store also sold liquor.

Upon entering the store, I quickly scanned the liquor aisle and purchased a pint of gin, a magazine, and some snacks. In my mind this was going to be my last drink. I was moving to San Diego, California to get my life back on track. A change of venue is exactly what I needed. In recovery, we call it a geographical cure which is not necessarily effective unless one changes their thinking.

"Wherever I go, there I am."

When my bus finally arrived for boarding, I hugged my mother real close and sadly felt the warm tears come streaming down her brown cheek. I looked her in the eyes and told her how much I loved her. I promised that I was going to change for the better. I kissed her wet cheek and thanked her for everything. My mother waved to me until the bus faded into the distance. I waved back and blew her kisses.

The feeling of leaving my mother and not ever seeing her again almost wrecked my brain. I peered out the window at the scenery and saw that we hadn't reached the Mass Turnpike entry ramp. I momentarily contemplated stopping the bus and getting off, but what good would that do? I cracked open my bottle of gin to enjoy a long comforting swig. The boy sitting next to me watching was too young to offer a sip, so I placed the bottle carefully back into the bag then secured it between my waist and armrest for easy access.

By the time the bus reached the border of Massachusetts and Connecticut, I was stone cold drunk and had accepted an invitation to switch seats further in the rear of the bus where the action was. I joined a group of four white dudes who were about my age chilling in the back of the bus playing a radio and drinking their own booze. I partied with these cool cats until we reached the transfer point in Manhattan.

When I lived in Syracuse, New York, I used to frequent Manhattan, so I was a little familiar with the Forty-Second Street terrain.

I departed the Port Authority Bus Depot, crossed the street to the nearest liquor store and purchased a bottle of beer and a pack of cigarettes. Further down Forty-Second Street, I located a crack dealer whose clean hustling attire dispelled most trust issues. I walked up to the man and handed him a twenty dollar bill and in exchange he handed me back seven vials of crack which he spit out of his mouth. The transaction lasted a milli-second. Both of us quickly departed the area going separate ways.

Afterwards, I proceeded to find myself a secluded place to get high so I walked into an X-rated theater where I came across a feenin crack addict holding a crack pipe. We both sat down in a movie booth and got stoned. I even shared a bottle of beer with him so we could mellow out the high. This is common behavior which I later learned is polysubstance abuse or maladaptive behavior; mixing deferent substances to achieve a certain desired affect. After we finished smoking the crack,

I handed the dude a couple of bucks for the road and found my way back into the Port Authority bus station to check up on my bus schedule.

To my dismay, the transfer bus was going to be delayed another hour. What was I going to do for an hour, I wondered. I glanced across the bus terminal with the wide eyes and gritted teeth of a person high on crack. I spotted those same four white dudes from the bus ride there. I scurried on over to them and asked, "What's up?"

The tall red-headed guy took one look at me and excitedly mouthed, "Hey dude, you're stoned!" He asked if I could cop some more. Without delay I took their money and made another trip back to the same dealer who was still hanging on Forty-Second Street, but this time I copped enough drugs and alcohol for the five of us.

After boarding our bus, we partied like rock stars. We partied until the bus arrived in Indiana. By then, the bus driver was tired of our constant disturbances and had called ahead to the terminal to complain. When we arrived at the station, we were met by an armed posse of Indiana police officers who forced us off the bus, then instructed us to get sober and catch the next bus ride headed for San Diego.

We hung around the city for an hour before I realized that I had not eaten all day. I had spent all my money partying and still had over two days left on the road. For the remainder of the bus ride, I was going to have to steal food in order to eat. At one rest stop, even though I was hungry, I wound up stealing a quart of beer instead of food.

I generalized my behavior by thinking that beer is nothing but barrel and hops, which in itself is food.

The remainder of the trip was uneventful. I sat quietly watching the awesome desert landscapes day-dreaming of one day being sober and able to live with my wife and children again. Finally, the bus arrived in downtown San Diego in the early evening, and I was picked up by my big brother, Jr.

We hadn't seen each other for many years and displayed that affection with a long, loving embrace. To me, my brother still looked the same, tall, and handsome. I'm sure that he couldn't say the same for me. He patted me on my shoulder then said,

"Come on l'il brother. Let's get you cleaned up."

My brother drove a blue Honda Civic and on our way to his house, he gave me the 411 on what was going on in his life.

Jr. was in the Navy and lived with his family on the Nas Marimar Naval Air Station. This base is noted for the filming location of the movie "Top Gun" starring Tom Cruise. The ride was a thirty-five minute drive from downtown. When we arrived at the house, I was lovingly greeted at the door by my sister-in-law, two nieces, and nephew who were eagerly excited to have Uncle Stone come to visit them. After receiving such a positive, loving welcome, I felt that I was on the right track to getting my life back together.

I did not know, or understand, that wherever I went, there was no escaping myself. If I was going to succeed, I needed to change my negative way of thinking, to a positive, more prosocial way.

The very next day my family took me clothes shopping at an area mall. They purchased me an entire new wardrobe, and then instructed me to throw out my worn, ripped, smelly clothes. I discovered later that my dear mother had financed the whole venture with hopes that this will help me get my life together. While we were shopping, my criminal mind noticed the lax in security which made me compare how these stores were nothing like the stores in the cities that I was used to stealing from. Here there was no visible security at all.

I found myself pushing the shopping cart from one department to another with half-full shopping bags of the things we previously purchased. There were no security guards following me or waiting around to prevent me from filling the bags to capacity. Unsuspecting to my family, while we browsed, I began placing additional items in the bags.

Jr. didn't notice my additional items until we got home and saw me tapping the crystal to my new Quartz watch that I had just stolen. I also showed him the rest of my treasures. I figured he wouldn't be bothered since he was also raised in corrupt Boston.

Jr. was definitely unprepared for anything else I was capable of getting into. He helped me obtain a job as a short order cook off base where he worked part-time.

The place was a student center located on the campus of the International Business University in Scripps Ranch. I was employed as a short order cook and cashier for yuppie students who traveled from all around the world to attend business classes at the University. Situated outside opposite patio doors, there were two swimming pools always loaded with tanning students who often entered the center to order food or play video games dripping wet and young women wearing thongs. "This place is a gangster's paradise," I thought.

My brother and I were the only two workers who ran the center. In addition to the good pay, I had the run of the place. Things became more lucrative once I learned how to scam the monetary system. Every shift that I worked, the first fifty-dollars in purchases that came across the counter had gone directly into my pockets.

Alcoholic beverages were not sold at the Center and when I discovered that there were no drugs in the area, I started to travel by long bus ride to the city just to get high on weekends. Those runs later turned into weeknights. My brother quickly noticed the patterns of my behavior and became irritated at me for being a screw up, and for constantly drinking alcoholic beverages around his children. In addition, I was arriving home late hours of the night. I was a poor role model for my nieces and nephews.

My brother confronted me on the matter and our discussion turned into a physical confrontation. He shoved me, but I ignored his advances because I loved my brother and did not want to hurt him. He jumped on me, knocked me down, and choked me almost unconscious before his wife yelled for him to let go of my throat. After that threatening episode, I knew I had to move from his house quickly because I began contemplating whether or not I was going to let him live. With haste I packed my belongings, and then hitched a ride to downtown San Diego where I could be with addicts and alcoholics like me. They understood me.

To my dismay, downtown San Diego at night could be compared to a third-world country. It didn't resemble any place I had ever visited before. There were literally hundreds of homeless men and women, young and old, sprawled out on top of tainted, dirty card board boxes laid out on the sidewalks for blocks. Each morning at five a.m., just before the work day began they would be ushered off to the outskirts of town by police. Then sanitation workers would hose down the sidewalks where drunk and high, destitute, suffering, human bodies previously lay.

Before this, I never imagined that this much suffering existed in the world's most powerful and richest nation. I considered it an unattended human crisis. It sparked some deep resentments and anger in me towards our leaders. Crack cocaine was so abundant that ten-dollars would buy me what I spent thirty-dollars for back home in Boston. Not only was it plentiful, the effects were much stronger. The high was very intense but lasted for a shorter period and it drove me insane. I met men and women who had not smoked crack for days, but still appeared zombie-like with wide-eyes and gritting teeth as if they had just taken a hit. Predictably, it wasn't long before I became a part of those downtown fixtures.

Just like the rest, I got drunk and high and fell out on the sidewalks, sleazy motels, under bridges, in cardboard boxes and apartment hallways. I was strung out like an animal exhibit on the neatly trimmed lawn of the World Famous San Diego Zoo in Balboa Park. I also slept on the steps of area churches.

The line for sleeping in the homeless shelter was three days long. Unless I was employed, I was only allowed to stay three nights.

To support my addiction, sometimes I performed day labor at construction sites, emptied cargo at truck stops, pulled off petty heists, or sold dummy crack rocks to unsuspecting addicts. That scam got me beat up a couple of times. The police were always stopping and frisking me. It was only a matter of time before they caught me with some drugs. I thought if the streets were this mean then I really do not want to visit the harsh realities of the San Diego jail. I'd probably have to join a gang in order to survive. It was not very long before I ended up selling everything I owned, which my concerned mother bought for me - my clothes, shoes, and jewelry. All I had left was the outfit I wore and an exchange in a dirty shoulder bag.

After enduring this brutal self-inflicted treatment for a couple of months, I knew I couldn't last like some of the homeless people who have lived that way for many years. I signed myself into the three-day detox program located on Market and 12th Street. It felt really comforting to finally take a hot shower and get some sleep in a clean, warm bed. The food at the establishment was very nutritional. In just those three days there were noticeable, beneficial changes in my appearance and attitude. After completing the three day detox, I decided to continue my recovery and voluntarily signed into the Salvation Army Rehabilitation Center on Broadway Street. The center hosted a six-month recovery program with guaranteed employment upon completion. The quiet atmosphere there allowed me to hear myself think. I needed that. This program was extremely intense which compelled me to search deep within myself. But…

I was in fear of what I might find.

All the groups required full participation. Unlike any other program I had attended up to that point, in this program we were required to work eight hours a day in addition to attending the groups. The groups consisted of orientation, substance abuse, relapse prevention, meditation, and AA/NA meetings outside the facility in the evening. It appeared to be a very effective program, but one thing made me uncomfortable was the huge emphasis the program director placed on work over the core rehabilitation component.

Each week I was allotted a small ten dollar stipend for my forty hours of constant work. I worked unloading docks, lifting heavy items like refrigerators, furniture, boxes, etc.; items which were ultimately sold in their stores. I mysteriously wondered where all this money I made for the program was going.

One day, I got the opportunity to ask that question to the director personally. In response, he peered at me through shifty blue eyes with putrid disdain, as if to call me an ungrateful scumbag, and walked off without even answering my question. Later on that early evening, I watched from my dorm window as the director, wearing his immaculate Salvation Army uniform drove away from the beige brick building in a polished new red Lincoln Town Car. Anger built up inside me, but I dismissed any notions I had to leave the program right away.

I actually felt that I was making some progress with my recovery, and enjoyed the work environment. I enjoyed

Donald R. Frye

attending groups and meetings with people like myself who were trying to get well. In addition, I was aware that one of the eight females in the program was attracted to me. I wanted to see where that would lead. For the first thirty-days at this program I was restricted to the building and had been required to give random urine tests and ingest daily doses of Antibuse.

Antibuse is a medicine that causes an allergic reaction if I were to come in contact with any alcoholic substances.

This prescribed order prevented me from sneaking any drinks. After my thirty-day restriction ended, I went for my first walk alone and tested the waters of sobriety. Like an insane man, I definitely walked straight down Market Street, which was the heart beat of the crack monster. I passed through the beast unscathed by the temptation to use. But, on my next walk a week later, I wasn't as successful and took a couple of hits of crack. Somehow, someway, I managed to maintain my composure. I waited to cool down before entering the rehab building where I succeeded with evading detection from the desk manager or anyone else from the program for the entire night.

The very next day in group, I felt really insincere and guilty because I had cheated. I wanted to confide in somebody, but I did not want to get suspended from the program. There was no one I could trust with my secret. It was tearing me apart inside. A week had lapsed before I attempted to go back out alone.

But this time, I didn't make it back!

I got high and quickly returned to the life of the living dead. Still conscious of the fact that I was supposed to wait a week to allow the Antibuse to leave my system, within two days, I began to drink alcohol and became very ill. After just one drink, I began to experience severe flu-like symptoms and could not even make it to a hospital. In a bout for survival, I struggled to the outskirts of town, broke into an apartment building where I climbed the stairs to the roof and laid down in a tight fetal position then shivered myself to sleep. The next morning, I awoke with my pants soiled and shirt soaked in sickly sweat. Yet, I felt better and well rested.

I exited the apartment building and walked the few blocks to Broadway Street where I took a quick bath, fully clothed, in a huge public fountain outside the San Diego

Civic Center. I did not even care who was watching or what others were thinking.

My impoverished tormented soul was completely lost and turned out.

I was very distant from my spiritual core and just wanted it all to end. My arrogant, cowardly self prevented me from committing suicide. Instead I opted for the inevitable slow agonizing death that usually results from self-inflicted alcohol and drug abuse.

For the next few months, I pan handled my way around San Diego and sold plasma twice a week. This is how I had discovered I had contracted the Hepatitis-C virus. Later, with treatment, I was cured of this infection. I committed petty thefts and even prostituted myself a couple of times.

My mental condition was rapidly deteriorating.

I no longer cared to exist.

My only goal was to stay drunk and I would do anything to achieve it. I began getting into more frequent fist fights with people I didn't even recognize as my victims. I also became the victim taking some brutal poundings. I was once held hostage overnight by four armed and dangerous thugs who considered holding me until a big-time drug dealer arrived.

Initially, I tried to fight my way out of it but was stomped to the ground. I laid down in a ball trying to cover my head and face as best as I could. When the drug dealer finally showed up, I recognized him as someone who I had robbed for some crack and money. Once this man saw my face, he rushed into the room and punched me straight in the mouth, swelling my top lip. Instantly, I saw my life flash before my eyes. I scanned the room for an escape route, but there was none. I was out-numbered five-to-one and completely surrounded. They forced me into a chair that stood in the middle of the living room of the apartment and they all looked at me with their fists balled tight and menacing looks.

Unexpectedly, the drug dealer began preaching to me. He stated that I was a good hustler and that he's watched me in action, but also noted that the alcohol and drugs had my mind twisted. Without warning, he suddenly reached his hands into his pockets, causing me to flinch and prepare myself for a brutal beating. Instead of hitting or shooting me, the drug dealer pulled out a thick wad of money, peeled off some bills, then handed them to me. I was in utter shock as he ordered my hesitant hands to take the money in a manner I couldn't refuse. Afterwards he instructed his thugs to drive me over to detox. He ordered me to get cleaned up for ten-days and they'll pick me up afterwards to work off my debts.

I believed it was divine intervention that I was still alive! Not only was I alive, but alive with two hundred dollars in my pocket. The thugs did as ordered and dropped me off at the detox center.

I walked through those doors with other plans in mind.

When they were gone, I left that building and went to purchase a bus ticket to Syracuse, New York. I had just made my dramatic escape from San Diego, California.

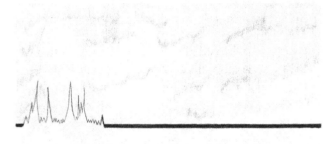

EXTREMITY

by
store '09'

Chapter

Six

EXTREMITIES

The Greyhound bus departed San Diego just in the nick of time!

While waiting for the bus to Syracuse to arrive, I decided to brave the dangerous drug-infested streets of downtown San Diego one more time to pick up supplies for my long trip. I had just finished purchasing some liquor and copping some crack cocaine when I was spotted by the armed street thugs who had kidnapped me and dropped me off at the detox program. They spotted me, but I was too quick and ran and hid until my bus arrived. While I was hiding, I took a hit off the crack pipe and a good swig of alcohol to calm my nerves.

Once safely on the bus, I was on my way to Syracuse to sign into another detox and rehab program. This time, as with all the other times, I was seriously convinced that I had had enough. I managed to buy myself some crack and booze for the trip. When the crack was finished, I flushed the glass stem down the commode. I promised myself, once again, that this was going to be my last time getting high. Afterwards, I got drunk and fell asleep.

When I awoke, the bus was cruising through the Arizona desert. The desert appeared dry and vast, yet colorful with visible signs of life. We traveled past occasional groups of cacti or tumble weeds, slow drifting in light scorching breeze. Before the bus could reach the Arizona bus terminal in Phoenix, I had befriended a young kid who claimed to be heading northeast.

We had been informed that the bus would stop at the terminal for servicing causing a half-hour delay. The delay would give us enough time to get some beer and scout out some weed to carry us through our journey.

My recent promise to myself never entered my thoughts.

We arrived in Arizona and the young kid pitched in fifty-bucks for the supplies, but insisted that he stay behind while I went searching. Of course, I was okay with that and I proceeded out of the terminal. I tipped up a busy street and located a grocery store. When I came to the isle containing the plastic sandwich bags, I scanned the isle for security, ripped open a box and pocketed a few bags.

I made my way undetected to the seasoning isle and pocketed a bottle of sweet basil. This occurrence from start to finish took ten minutes. I found my way back to the bus terminal just in time to meet the kid for boarding our bus. I handed the kid the plastic bag containing the herbs and told him I had changed my mind and decided to board a different bus going into Dallas, Texas. Without checking, the kid quickly pocketed the herbs and boarded the bus. Nothing I did was rehearsed. I had played out the entire scam by ear. I thought, "What's the rush? I'll just hang out here in Phoenix for a few." I'll check out the sights, and then catch a later departure.

I walked out the terminal and approached a man that looked like he knew his way around the hot spots of town. I asked him where they were. He gave me some directions to a motel about ten blocks from the terminal and pointed me towards the numbered transit bus that would take me there. When I arrived on the scene, things were already in full swing. The weather was extremely hot, the thermometer read 105 degrees. Prostitutes pranced up and down the boulevard wearing swim suits, thongs, and high heels.

I introduced myself to another crack fiend who easily directed me to a motel room with a long line of people waiting to purchase crack. The stairwell was insanely crowded with addicts feenin to get high. I was about the twenty-fifth person waiting in that long line. The crowd moved rapidly.

When I finally reached the threshold of the motel room, I was escorted inside by two armed thugs who pointed me towards two other armed thugs sitting at a table completely covered with pre-packaged drugs. I handed one of the men eighty-bucks and in exchange, I was handed a large rock of crack the size of a ping-pong ball. Another thug escorted me out a back door, down a staircase, and out of the building. Once outside, I met up with a female addict who brought me to her shack, which was also sprawling with crack fiends. I wasn't the least bit worried. This was my element.

I had grown used to navigating amongst these types of crowds. I was one of them. When the crack was finished, I sent the lady out to purchase more and I stayed at this roach infested place until I was completely broke. Once my pockets were void of anything but lint, it was time for me to go. I didn't even save any money for fare to get me back downtown, so I had to travel there on foot hoping to run into an easy victim. The walk towards town was long and tedious in the heat of the Arizona desert. I witnessed things that made me cringe and wanted to leave this town as soon as possible before I got stuck or put in a position as I was while in San Diego. When I arrived at the terminal, it was a coincidence that my bus heading northeast was ready for boarding.

I entered the coach looking like a crack-crazed monster reeking of alcohol, drugs and funk. I must have scared whomever I sat next to and made them feel very uncomfortable. When my body finally stopped tweaking, I was able to sleep through most of Arizona.

When we reached Dallas, Texas with a short delay, I went outside the station for some fresh air. Across from the station I spotted some good Samaritans feeding the hungry and homeless out of their van. I thought God must be watching over me as I instantly hopped into that line to receive my portion of charitable delicacies. After the crowd died down, I spoke to those good people and explained my travel dilemma to them. After hearing my story, they gave me some extra sandwiches to sustain me for the remainder of my long journey.

When I re-entered the bus terminal, I went to the ticket agent and traded my ticket to Syracuse for a bus headed right into Boston. It was the same fare. I came to the conclusion that I wanted to be close to home and enter into yet another program. The long cross-country trip to Boston became a detox itself. For the next two and a half days, I ate sandwiches and slept. I almost slept through having the chance at viewing one of the worlds' Great Lakes while traveling through Minnesota towards New York.

I arrived in Boston the spring of 1991 and went and checked myself into the Framingham Detox Center. Afterwards, I reported to Long Island Shelter holding program which housed fifty beds for men and twenty-five for women seeking recovery. During my stay there, I entered a voluntary employment program. After establishing a good work history the program director selected me for a position at the world-renowned Brigham and Women's Hospital. For once in my adult life, I was making some positive and constructive progress.

I was sober and employed. Something I hadn't been since I was fourteen years old.

Unfortunately, this didn't last long.

Everything came to an abrupt end the day I received my first pay check. After visiting the check cashier, I was off and running and never went back to work. I had embarrassed my employers, who hardly knew me, but still trusted and believed in me enough to place their professional images on the line for me. I felt really guilty but the urge to feed my addiction was stronger. Once again, I was caught out there trying to stay sober on my own without any support system. Because of this, I ended up back on the streets sleeping in crack houses.

One particular lucky day I called my mother on the phone to check on how she was doing. To my surprise, she informed me that arrangements were made for my oldest daughter, Elizabeth, to come visit her for the summer. I was very excited about the news. I hadn't seen my baby since 1987! Since the time we had departed on such very bad terms. Knowing my baby was coming to Boston, I checked myself into the volunteer prisoner detox program, again! I wanted to get cleaned up for my baby's arrival.

After signing in, I devoured everything that was served on the prison menu and visited the gym to lift weights.

During my stay, I did not attend any NA/AA meetings or groups. I was using this program as a pit stop. When I completed the detox, I went over to my mother's house and it was a great surprise and awesome feeling when I saw my baby. She screamed, "Daddy!" She ran and jumped into my arms!

It was a moment that I wished could have lasted forever.

"My Elizabeth," I whispered in her ear as we embraced for what seemed like hours. That evening I managed to stay sober and we enjoyed doing family things. The three of us ate dinner at a Chinese restaurant, The Yellow Dragon, which was located on American Legion Highway in Roslindale. Afterwards, we came home and strolled down memory lane while looking through our family albums.

The same evening we received a phone call from my wife Rhonda, whom I hadn't spoken to for many years. After a brief greeting, she placed our youngest daughter Trudy on the phone. My young daughter heard my voice and began to cry. She stated that she wanted to come home to see her daddy, too. I was touched emotionally, I had to explain to my daughter how I couldn't afford to send for her at that moment and I made a promise for another time.

My dear mother, after hearing our conversation, somehow managed to make Trudy's wish come true. Her clothes were packed and she was flown to Boston the very next day. This was an awesome moment for us all. I had both my babies physically in my life.

All I needed to do was maintain my sobriety. I was actually doing quite well for a couple of weeks.

One sunny afternoon, my two daughters and I were in the back yard picking fruit from a plum tree when a friend of mine drove up into the driveway in a dark blue sedan. I excused myself from my daughters to speak with my friend. After a five-minute conversation, I waved to my daughters and promised them that I would be right back. After leaving, both of my daughters gave my friend a chilling stare as if to say, "Don't ever come back here again. You spoiled our wonderful moment with our daddy."

Scooter was a drug dealer who was looking for a safe place where he could process and package some drugs. I knew from past experiences with him that by catering to his needs that I would earn some quick dollars in very little time, so we drove off. We rode around the corner to an empty house that my mother owned. As soon as we entered the home and I saw those drugs, my stomach began churning, mind racing, and beads of sweat poured down my forehead. Just like a laboratory rat, Scooter used me to test the drugs for potency. After finishing his business, he handed me some dollars and a package of cocaine then drove me back to my mother's place where my daughters awaited my return.

They took one look at me and instantly noticed the change in my character. At the time, my daughters were age five and eight and keenly observant, and knew me very well. I had been transformed into a 'Schitzo-maniac' with my eyes dotting from here to there. It didn't seem fit for me to play with my daughters anymore. I left the house then joined back into the rat race. For the next two days, I drank and got high out of guilt for having left my girls. I needed them and knew that they needed me, so I signed myself, yes once again, back into the volunteer prisoner detox program for another ten days.

At this stage of my addiction, my life had become a complete mess. I troubled everyone around me. Before the end of the summer, I had fallen out with both my young daughters – again! I had managed to screw things up and this was the last time I saw them physically.

When the summer ended they were flown back to Minneapolis, via Delta Airlines, where they stayed with their mother. Once they were gone out of my life, I became extremely depressed and stayed drunk and high trying to subdue that pain. I continued in and out of detoxes using them as a means to survive or until something clicked in my mind that caused me to stay clean and sober. I signed into the Framingham, Somerville, Dimock Street, and Boston detoxes. I even voluntarily committed myself into a psychiatric hospital for experiencing suicidal ideas.

I felt the walls closing in on me.

Everybody was trying to hurt me

The streets were no longer safe for me. The only place I could travel without becoming extremely fearful was downtown Boston. It was sort of a neutral zone that was over populated with alcoholics and addicts, who like myself, would be killed if we were caught back in the hood. Our families and friends had dismissed us and all we had was each other.

After completing one detox program, I went to visit my mother who was clearly showing signs of failing health. She had developed lung cancer and had kept it from the family for as long as she could. I believe my mother concealed her illness because she did not want to worry us or be a burden. That was the kind of black woman she was; always putting her children's well being first, even if it meant denying herself. Sitting with her at home, I could see that she was very ill. I stayed all day at my mother's and we watched a few TV programs and I took the pleasure of weeding her tomato garden.

When my mother finally took a nap, that's when I made my slimy move. I stole her Sony Stereo speakers then went and traded them for drugs. The speakers were large and would be easily missed when she woke. I was a cowardly sick man full of self-hatred. I continued to put my dear mother through so much agony, especially for taking advantage of her when she was very sick.

That day when I left my mother's house with her stereo speakers was the last time I would see her alive!

I sold those speakers for a quarter of what they were worth, then went and got drunk and high. Afterwards I hid downtown at the homeless shelter for veterans.

After a few days had passed, I phoned home with the audacity to see how things were. This phone call gave my mother the chance to vent her frustrations. She told me how she truly felt about how my addiction was affecting her health. I was told never to come there again. After my mother spoke, the phone went silent except for the sound of deep shallow breathing as she gasped for breath.

I became angry at the truth in the words she had spoken, slammed down the receiver as if she had done something wrong to me. Then the saga continued.

I became more brazen while committing criminal offenses that could get me sent to prison. My life had completely spiraled out of control. I began visiting a psychiatrist on an out-patient basis, but after only three visits, he cancelled our sessions due to the fact that he could not effectively treat me if I couldn't stay sober. The doctor urged me to seek long term care. He went as far as to phone a few establishments to inquire if they could effectively treat my horrid condition and who would accept any Mass Health Insurance.

He located a hospital, AdCare, who accepted me and my healthcare insurance. I was now deemed disabled, diagnosed with chronic alcoholism and major depressive-affective disorders. I was classified as being dual diagnosed meaning I had chronic substance abuse issues and psychological manifestations. This made me ineligible for many programs because I was only able to be effectively treated if I was at a clinical establishment which dealt with both issues and in the surrounding area there weren't many. But it did make me eligible for disability benefits.

I checked into AdCare treatment facility which was a very clinical atmosphere. At this establishment, I had the luxury of group and individual therapy which allowed me to be open while sharing my feelings.

Regardless of whatever avenues I traveled, there always seemed to be some kind of void.

When I received my first retroactive disability check, which had been mailed to my mother's address, she deposited the nine-thousand dollars in the bank for me. I instructed her to accept six-thousand of those dollars as payback for the things I had stolen from her, but I knew deep in my heart that nothing material could ever restore any psychological damage I had caused her. With the constant gnawing that I had money available, I left the AdCare program prematurely and went on another excursion.

My mother was holding twenty-five hundred dollars of my three-thousand. It left me with five-hundred dollars that she sent to me through Western Union. First, I went clothes shopping, then to the liquor store to purchase some booze. I sat in the Boston Common, a historic scenic public park filled with tall trees, grassy lawn, strolling paths, street vendors, and ponds teaming with tourists. I found a secluded quiet spot and drank beer while contemplating my next move. My mind was gauging the city. I knew that there weren't many safe havens for me to go and get high. But I remembered that I knew a small group of guys who use to frequent the Long Island Shelter in Quincy. They now occupied rooms in a Brownstone near the world-renowned Massachusetts General Hospital.

This seemed to be the perfect spot for me to go, so I walked downtown to the hot spots and copped some crack. I traveled on foot to those brownstones to see what was going on with them dudes. To my lucky surprise, they were all home. I counted four men and a woman present and already indulging in drinking and smoking crack.

I was familiar with them all and was well aware that each and every one of them suffered from HIV or full-blown AIDS, but those dangers didn't stop me from sharing crack pipes and drinks with them. After taking a few hits, I noticed a couple of them began to get sick and began exchanging different medications with each other. My thoughts were on being the first one to grab their share of drugs if and when they fell out. A few hours had passed and I had run out of drugs and money.

By then they had all started to disrobe and make sexual advances toward one another. They still had money and some crack but refused to share with me unless I joined into their little orgy. I sat there at the table feenin while scraping minute traces of resin off the neck of the crack pipe. Grown men with full-blown AIDS were across the small room engaging in unclean sexual acts. They continued to try to entice me into their little orgy.

They even showered the scene with condoms. The urge to get high was strong and I was facing a very perverted and dangerous decision.

Somewhere in the confusion of my mind, my thoughts of getting high caused me to unbutton my shirt. Suddenly, one of the men stopped me and asked for me to follow him to get more drugs. What a relief, I thought as I snapped out of that haze and the two of us left the building. After purchasing some more drugs and booze, I asked the dude for a small piece of crack and we went our separate ways.

That summer evening, I stayed outside the entire night, and took a long nap on a grassy knoll of the Boston Public Garden. I awoke feeling rested. I walked the distance to the St. Francis House shelter just in time to catch breakfast.

From there, I went off hustling. With the first fruits of my labor, I purchased a bus ticket back to Syracuse, New York.

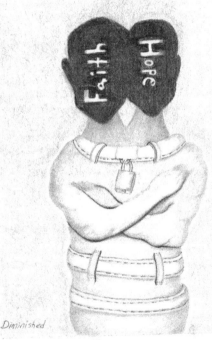

Diminished

by
Stone '04

Chapter

Seven

DIMINISHED

In mid-1991, I arrived back in Syracuse, New York. Upon my request, my mother sent me the twenty-five hundred dollars left over from my retroactive SSI check. I used this money to rent a cheap roach infested apartment on the North-East side of town. Later, I befriended a young lady, named CeeCee, who a few years prior, at the age of fourteen had given birth to a baby girl which she had given up for adoption. CeeCee had vast knowledge and experience with the street life but she didn't use drugs or drink alcohol and wasn't aware of what she would be getting involved with being my lady.

I was not too demanding of her but she made sure I kept money in my pockets, rent paid and nice clothes and jewelry to wear. She would go out any day of the week for a few hours, then return home and hand me all the money she would make. I thought things were going very well. I phoned my mother to ask for my wife Rhonda's phone number and address, but per my wife's orders I was not privy to this information. I informed my mother of my good intentions to reach out to them and send my daughters some money, but she only suggested that I mail the money to her and that she would see to it that they receive it. In my mind I wanted them to know that the money came from their daddy because I was always thinking about them.

When I realized that I couldn't convince her and was not getting my way, I mailed my mother a few hundred-dollars. I gave up trying to connect with my daughters for the moment. At this stage of my addiction, I weighed one hundred and twenty pounds. The thick gold chain that I wore draped around my slender neck resembled a noose. The gold ropes were almost as thick as my skinny neck even though I continue to believe that I was a fly sneaker pimp. After about six-months giving me all her money and watching me get stoned, CeeCee convinced herself that our situation wasn't going to change for the better.

It was actually getting worse. I began forcing her out. At the time, I was throwing my money out the window by feeding my addiction all the while sharing my alcoholic and junkie friends as well.

I was a pathetic pimp

The last straw for CeeCee came after she had gotten pregnant. I ordered her to go to Rochester, New York for an abortion. CeeCee never came back to my apartment. For two months I kept an ear to the ground in search of my cash cow but she was nowhere to be found. I had grown dependent on her and soon all my accumulated wealth began to dwindle. I began selling my jewelry and stereo. I once again became a destitute bum.

Just when I was about to lose my apartment, my luck changed. I was chosen by a young lady named Rose, whose only obsession was *me*. She didn't indulge in drugs or alcohol. Rose wasn't as street savvy as CeeCee, so I had to get out there in the streets to teach her what CeeCee actually taught me about the hoe game. Rose's performance received an okay grade. It wasn't long before we had a long list of johns' numbers for her to cater to. Whenever I needed money I sent her out. She wasn't like CeeCee who would just go out there. Often times, I used some mental or physical coaxing. I believed she resisted only to receive some attention from me because more often than not, my thoughts were stuck on getting high. I was sharing needles, shooting coke in my arms while taking hits off the crack pipe. I was also having unprotected sex with my prostitute girlfriend. Literally, it seemed I was trying to commit suicide with toxic combinations.

I discovered I had an increasing tolerance. With help from some friends, I was spending hundreds of dollars a day on alcohol and drugs. I was insane! The police began putting pressure on me. They would pick up Rose and try to convince her to turn on me, but she was loyal. Wow! The last thing I needed was a pimping charge.

Within a few months, Rose finally left me. She chose another pimp because all I did was spend my money drinking and getting high.

Throughout these times, I met other women who had their lives together. They wanted to be with a man of my stature and proportions, but I wasn't able to measure up to their pro-social demeanor. I left them alone because I no longer wanted to bring these women down to my level of ignorance as I did my wife. But, if they were already lost and turned out then I would let them cater to me.

Rose leaving me led to my getting back to hustling on the streets. It wasn't long before I stopped paying rent and was evicted.

Once again, I found myself visiting the rescue mission's drunk tank. This time it only took me about seven different visits of sleeping in the tank before reaching the decision to participate in the extended recovery program. I mainly used this program for a safe and clean place to rest and gather my thoughts.

First, I detoxed for five days. I then signed into the thirty-day treatment program in East Syracuse. This was another intense program equipped with on-board psych medications and psychiatrist. I was prescribed Depacote for my depression. I also enjoyed the benefits of the one-on-one counseling and group therapy.

We were allowed to gather together as a group for support while we confronted our issues. For instance, if someone believed or felt that their addiction stemmed from an action of a family member who hurt them then that person unsuspecting to the individual would be brought into the group for them to confront. We also would place a recovering person in a chair located in the center of our circle called the hot seat. The group would be invited to ask questions and give positive feedback, concerning their character defects and addiction. I was crafty enough to rationalize my behaviors and fool the group into believing that my issues were not that serious.

I met the greatest bunch of men and women at this program. Together we shared laughter and many tears. It was a victorious, but sad day when we completed the program and had to move on to our separate lives.

During this time I had managed to save up two months worth of my SSI checks. It was enough for a month's rent in my own room. When I graduated from the thirty-day recovery program I was assigned a bed in the extended recovery program at the rescue mission. I figured I would stay there and wait for an opening in a halfway or sober house.

I arrived looking and feeling very optimistic about life. My deep depressive mood had disappeared. It was late afternoon when I arrived. Everyone was attending groups or meetings. I stored my belongings in my assigned area, made my bed, and decided to take a trip to the mall to purchase some clothing and other items, but as soon as I departed that building with a pocket full of money the hold of my addiction kicked in. With no support system, such as a sponsor or someone I could get in touch with, the urge to use hit me hard. I immediately picked up where I left off and was back out there amongst the living dead. I began drinking, drugging, and scamming people in order to fuel my addiction. I truly hated myself for messing up all these opportunities that were given to me.

Every time I thought I'd hit rock bottom, I found that I could go even deeper.

I listened and shared in groups and attended AA/NA meetings.

What was it going to take for me to get clean and stay clean?

For many years now, I've just been scraping myself off the rock hard surface of the bottom. My mind was saturated with perverted thoughts and my body beaten and bruised. So now I wondered what, where, and when this self-inflicted agony was going to end. An even more important question was - How?

Will I get shot or killed?

Stabbed?

Diseased?

I had no idea how my life was going to end but I felt that it was going to be a tragic one if I continued to drink and use drugs in this fashion. I often worried about leaving behind a bad legacy for my grandchildren. The last straw for me came and went on another evening.

I was stalking the downtown streets looking for a victim, when Syracuse's finest pulled up beside me in a police cruiser. The officer on the driver's side rolled down his window and asked me for identification. I responded by asking him if I had done something wrong. My inquiry caused the officers to park the cruiser. Both of them quickly jumped out of the car and approached me in an aggressive manner.

I sucker punch the first one who reached me. They wrestled me to the ground, bruising me until they handcuffed me and threw me into the rear of the police cruiser. They hauled me off to the public county jail.

Once in the building, I was ushered into a small cage and asked some questions. I was shown some photos of other people. My sarcastic responses got me beat up pretty darn good. I said if I did know these people, which I didn't, what makes you think I'd tell. Suddenly, I was blind folded from behind. The room went dark and I was kicked and punched over my entire body including my face and head.

When the blind fold was removed, I was violently pushed back into a chair and then shown these same photos. This time, I responded with a made up story of how I seen those guys frequenting the shelter on the Southside of town. The truth of the matter was I did not recognize any of the people in the photos. I also did not want to have to spend the night in jail sober.

My nose was bleeding profusely, so one of the officers threw me a rag to wipe my face. Then a brusque looking detective handed me his business card and told me to call him if I see or hear anything of interest. The nerve of these chumps I thought as they kicked me out the side door of the building.

This degrading exchange took no more than thirty minutes. My nose hurt and continued to bleed, so I walked to the St. Joseph hospital to get it checked out. The doctor confirmed that my nose was in fact broken. The receptionist scheduled me for a follow-up appointment to a nose specialist. The specialist was trained to reset my nose back in place. By this time it was 2 a.m. This took up most of my night.

I was feenin for a hit of crack and shaking because I hadn't tasted any alcohol all day. Except for a few dust balls of lint, my pockets were totally devoid of anything of value. All the regular stores that I hustled from to get me off empty were closed. All except for the twenty-four hour store. So I planned on stopping there to hang out front to see what kind of action materialized.

As I walked towards the store, I decided to detour so I could case out a factory near the highway overpass. I swiftly checked to see if there were any alarms on the windows. After reassuring myself, I used a brick to bust through a small pane of glass and slid my thin frame into the building. Once inside, I grabbed a bag and packed some items that I knew would sell easily on the Spanish west side. On the way out, climbing back through the same window, I cut my knee very deep on a sharp edge of glass. Instantly my blood began spewing in every direction, so I used my snot rag to try and stop the bleeding.

After locating a safe place to hide my treasure, I limped back to the hospital to get my knee stitched up. By the time the hospital staff finished giving me ten stitches, it was four a.m. almost daylight. Now with a bandaged leg, broken nose, and black eye, I retrieved my goods and limped over to the Spanish west side of town hoping to get any kind of deal possible at this time of morning.

What I didn't expect was to get robbed. I was jacked by two scraggly thugs who pinned me down and took my bag full of goods. They kicked me a few times for good measure before running off. Frustrated, I rose to my feet, brushed off, then walked over to the rescue mission drunk tank to sleep it off. But because I wasn't drunk, I wasn't allowed in.

It was around six in the morning. I was very tired and my body was engulfed in pain. I had nowhere else to go. After giving some thought, I walked the long distance and entered the greyhound bus terminal. I sat down and dozed off for a few hours. I awoke to the sounds of a lively crowd of travelers and instantly switched into scam mode.

After scamming a man by selling him forty dollars worth of fake weed, it was finally time to feed my addiction. It had never occurred to me that I hadn't eaten or that I was still in pain from the prior evening events. My mind and body needed drinks and drugs.

After feeding my addiction, my body began to feel as if it was about to collapse. I was worn out, exhausted, so I walked back to the drunk tank. It was a surprise to the medical staff because it was only mid-afternoon. They were only used to me showing up there oblivious at three of four in the morning.

I warned the staff that this was it for me, I had reached my bottom.

"I can't do this anymore!" I exclaimed.

"I've scraped the bottom long enough. Please help me!" I pleaded.

My body was in such decrepit shape that the medical staff required me to detox for seven days before admitting me back into the extended recovery program.

At this moment in time, I felt serious about my recovery. I remained at this program for one month. It was the cleanest time ever since first picking up a drink or drug. During my stay in the recovery unit, I was being educated on the effects of substance abuse. We believed that I was definitely making some significant strides. I even had a potential candidate chosen as my sponsor. I listened intently in groups, studied, and completed all the homework assignments.

At one point, I was required to write about what I think of what I would have become if I had not chosen the life style of an alcoholic and addict. This assignment, a first of its kind for me, was very interesting. It caused me to really take a thorough peek at my character traits. Also, during my stay I made frequent calls to my mother whose physical condition was drastically deteriorating. After meeting with the counselors a few times, I decided that I really needed to be home with my ailing mother. To my surprise, I was given a farewell, sent off with best wishes and hopes for me and my family. What beautiful people I thought.

I arrived at the bus terminal, where I used the pay phone to call and inform my mother that I was at the bus station and on my way home. My mother had answered the phone sounding very lethargic. She informed me that the doctors began prescribing her morphine to numb the pain.

Donald R. Frye

Instead of thinking the worse for my ailing mother, the word "morphine" caused a bell to ring in my brain and stomach to bubble. That feeling was my addiction kicking into gear. After that telephone conversation I proceeded to the ticket counter and purchased a one-way ticket to Boston.

The time was 11 o'clock in the morning. The bus departing for Boston wouldn't be leaving until three o'clock, four hours later. I walked to a corner store and purchased one beer without once even considering everything I just learned at the recovery program. I sat there in deep thought about my mother's condition. When the alcohol took effect, I mouthed to myself, "What the heck? I have a few hours to kill before the bus leaves." I had an eight hour journey to sleep it off. I walked the distance to the south side projects where I rented a drug den and bought some crack to smoke. The three o'clock bus departure had come and gone. I was stuck in that drug den getting high spending all my money that I had saved up while in rehab.

None of those group lessons or one-on-one therapeutic sessions even entered my thoughts. When I was completely broke, I left that filthy stinking shack and went and traded my bus ticket in for cash, convincing myself I would just get high some more. I could buy another ticket and leave for Boston the following morning.

This binge lasted for three entire days. I slithered in and out of that crack den. I'd go steal or scam someone of value and hurry back to that place of evil. Finally, I grew tired and my body was worn out. I couldn't handle anymore abuse. That is when I had concluded that it was time for me to go home.

The thought of getting high off my mother's morphine had also crossed my mind. After jostling up enough cash for another bus ticket, I phoned home again to let my mother know that I was on my way. The phone rang threw times before it was answered by my sister Greta who was sobbing on the other end when she informed me that our dear mother was dead. I boarded the next bus mystified and angry at myself, I arrived home within eleven hours.

I rang the door bell and my sister Greta answered the door. Her appearance and close resemblance to our mother had freaked me out. She was sobbing uncontrollably so I held her close to me until we both felt comforted. Later on that day we joined together with our oldest brother, Jr. who had flown in from Virginia Beach, Virginia, his new home. Then the three of us went to see our departed mother's body and prepare her funeral arrangements. The moment when I first glanced at our mother lying there in the casket, what I witnessed made me feel very sad. She was only fifty-five years old. How could this be?

From my past experiences with wakes and funerals, the dead usually look well rested and at peace. My mother, very thin with a death weight of sixty-five pounds, on the other hand, had this angry resentful smirk on her face.

I believed that look was meant for me. For the rest of my life, I'll never forget that look. My mother had worked very hard all her life to provide for us. She sacrificed everything for me. I paid her back by stealing from her, shaming her name and disrespecting her. This great black woman continued to love and believe in me, but my addiction wouldn't even allow me to make it home in time to comfort my mother in her final extremely painful moments. That disturbing look on her face was meant for me. It said, "Donald, you're an animal! You'll burn in Hell!"

After our two other brothers Tootie and Rusty showed up, we as a family laid *'mummy'* as we called her to her final resting place. "No Mummy, I yelled out to her casket. Get up! Get up!" How could this be?

For the five of us, it was a sad unifying moment. We hadn't been in the same room together since the 1970's. However we managed to keep in contact from time to time. After reading of our mother's will, my sister Greta traveled back to Atlanta where she lived. My brothers and I agreed to invest our inheritance proceeds together on a home and business in Virginia Beach, Virginia.

Donald R. Frye

Chapter

Eight

ROCK

BOTTOM

Jr., Rusty, and I had packed all of our mother's belongings into a medium-sized U-Haul truck. We traveled down I-95 south to Virginia Beach, Virginia. Our brother Tootie, planned to meet us there later. He first had to return to Syracuse and pack his belongings. During the entire trip, we remained silent, all trapped in fond memories of our dearly departed mother. I couldn't share the driving because every fifteen minutes or so, I broke out sobbing uncontrollably. The hurt of such a huge loss had a drastic effect on me. I never got a chance to say goodbye to the woman who gave birth to me.

We entered Virginia, crossing over the Chesapeake Bay Bridge. It is an awesome man-made structure that probably took a decade to complete. Jr's family house was located in Virginia Beach within a working class neighborhood of one-family homes. They lived in a beautiful four-bedroom home equipped with an attached garage and fireplace. They purchased it using both of their real estate credentials. Our plan was for Jr. and his wife to help

Rusty and me locate a good investment home.

Rusty and I were very close. He was two years older than me. We were always seen together. People thought we were twins. Growing up we participated together in various sports teams at the Roxbury boys and girls club of Boston. As a teenager, Rusty was awarded the best spring board diver in New England. But as we grew older we became chronic alcoholics.

At age 18, Rusty had joined the Air Force. During his service tour he began drinking alcohol very heavily. But in comparison, I thought that he was a functioning substance abuser. He wasn't nearly as bad as I was. His life was manageable. I was a self–destructive, chaotic type of substance abuser.

Our using together almost always ended up in turmoil. When I used, I became this happy-go-lucky person and Rusty became a miserable, depressed person. So while using, our relationship became strained.

When he drank he would become increasingly aggressive towards me, verbally first, but as time passed, he began taking advantage of my passive moods. He started shoving me around trying to agitate me into a physical confrontation. On the other hand, I was worse than him because my addiction never knew when to quit. I lived a very risky and dangerous lifestyle and often took risks while in Rusty's presence. I always gave him reasons to be angry at me.

I was a sneaky opportunist. When a victim presented themselves, I was always prepared to capitalize on their moment of weakness. In order to feed my addiction, I took chances that would place us in compromising situations. When we made it home, Rusty would cuss me out, but never stalled when reaching for a cut of my stolen treasures.

We both stayed at our brother Jr.'s house for about two months before finally locating and purchasing a good investment three bedroom home nearby. After we signed the papers and moved in, we arranged for our brother Tootie to move in from Syracuse. Now, there were three chronic drunks living under one roof. Shockingly, Tootie showed up in a friend's car with three cats, but he had no litter box for them to do their business in.

Immediately I knew that this mixture wasn't going to work out well. The situation reeked of disaster. The three of us were all mourning the loss of our mummy and we drank every day. Sometimes, we'd drink all day to subdue the pain from the void she left. It wasn't long before our brother Jr. joined the chorus and began stopping by our place to use our house as a spot to get high.

He'd stop by and get one of us to cop some crack and we would stay up most of the night getting high. All the while we'd be making plans for the janitorial franchise that we were joining. We had so many unsettled disagreements between us because there was no order, unity, or trust amongst us. Sometimes loud disputes would erupt and the disturbed neighbors would call the police.

When they arrived everyone would be calm except me. I would still be riled up from all the tension. A few times I became unruly with the police so they carted me off to jail for disturbing the peace. Eventually, we did get our janitorial franchise started and soon we were benefiting from a growing clientele.

One of our biggest clients owned an alcohol distribution center which was very convenient for us drunks. Almost every night we stole alcohol from the job site. There were stacks of cases everywhere. We found sample bottles of liquors from all around the world.

After all the cleaning was finished we'd arrive home around midnight. There stood ten bottles of different alcohol beverages from around the world, top shelf stuff covering our living room table. Sometimes if we had money, we'd stop off and cop some crack. Then the arguments would erupt about an hour after the first bottle of booze was cracked opened. By the time the booze was gone, I was in jail or outside lurking in the dark street shadows trying to avoid going to jail for fighting with my brothers.

Our spacious home sat on the banks of a long tributary of water that led to a lake. It was a beautiful, clean home only seven years old. Within six months, though, the place resembled something out of a western bar scene. The banisters, fixtures, and walls were broken during our fights and those three nasty cats were defecating and urinating on the carpets and the house became infested with their fleas. It was a horrendous scene.

I was fed up with living this way. I was spending too many late nights out wandering aimlessly through the unpredictable streets until my brothers fell asleep. Every night, my brother Rusty got drunk, he'd cuss me out and accuse me of killing our mother. He'd threaten to kill me. He'd also call me a lousy father and husband. He knew the right words to get my emotions riled up.

Every night my brother Tootie would take an hour or more singing Jimmy Hendricks's songs out loud until he fell asleep. My life had become a nightmare for sure. I no longer felt safe in my own home. Neither one of my brothers knew about or understood the hard, desperate turf that I had traveled.

My nightly walks began to get more brazen. I started breaking in to closed establishments and scamming people so that I could just get higher. It was as if I was chasing that euphoric feeling of that first drink or drug of the day. Again, this was another period of my active addiction where I was totally out of control. I needed a safe place to be where I could gather my thoughts.

I checked into Virginia Beach Seven-Day detox center. The rest and food had done me some good, but it didn't last long. After seven days, I ended up back home into the cesspool of alcohol, filth, and domestic violence. Nothing had changed.

One day, a drunken Rusty just sucker punched me in the face for no apparent reason. I responded back by picking up and throwing a glass jar full of ice and beer across the room at him. He ducked. Unintentionally, the glass jar smashed hard into the face of a visiting friend from New York. He was taken by ambulance to a hospital where he received multiple stitches. He later sued our insurance company. In addition, I was charged with assault and battery when the police arrived at the scene. I was jailed, but the charges were later dropped.

When I returned back from jail it was crazy business as usual. Things became so bad this time I signed back into detox hoping this time to gain entry to an extended substance abuse treatment program. As my luck would have it, there was an extensive waiting period before gaining entry into another program. I had no place to go that was clean and sober. No space became available to me so I was forced once again back to that house.

By this time, I had quit the janitorial business. I forfeited my shares because I knew that my looney brothers could never pay me back for my loss. The investments that I made with my mother's hard earned money and with my children in mind were forever lost. I grew deeply depressed and continued slugging the beer. I ended up going to jail for six months for borrowing our neighbor's car, which I rented to some drug dealers in exchange for some drugs. While in jail, I attended a substance abuse program, but I participated in them mainly to get housed into a cell block that was more tame than the rest.

I wasn't ready to quit this time. I had too much animosity and resentments towards my brothers. Everything I had shared in groups was insincere and the things that were said went in one ear, then out the other. So it was inevitable that when I got out I picked up where I left off. Time had just stood still as if I hadn't stopped for that period.

Soon after that episode, I ended up being committed into the Tidewater Emergency Psychiatric Ward for experiencing suicidal and homicidal thoughts. I was held as a patient there for thirty days and enjoyed the benefits of detox and stabilizing medication and some one-on-one counseling. When the sessions ended, I knew I needed more time, but I couldn't convince the medical staff to keep me longer. I even told them about my living situation with my brothers but they said they couldn't keep me and knew of no other place that would take me right away.

Now with nowhere else to go, I arrived back home to the front lines of a war zone. I became agitated and angry at myself for making the worse decision of my life to invest our mother's hard earned money with my idiot alcoholic brothers. I couldn't see any good coming out of our relationship or our business venture. This investment was going to be my chance to prove to my mother that I could do something positive and become successful like her. But now that was a dream deferred.

I grew so angry that I began to formulate a plan to kill them both by staging a house fire. Luckily for us all, I ended up committing myself back into the psychiatric hospital, but this time I urgently warned the hospital staff what would happen if I went back to that house.

I was going to kill all my brothers and myself, I exclaimed. The medical staff took my threats very seriously. They arranged to have me flown back to Boston where I could be treated by my original psychiatric doctor at Massachusetts General Hospital. Once I was safely away from my brothers, I went and stayed in the empty house that our mother had left to her sons.

Two months prior, the house had caught fire and had sustained significant electrical and smoke damage and it was deemed inhabitable by the fire Marshall. I moved in there anyway. The attic floors were burnt up and some of that debris had reached the second floor rooms which I cleaned up. I soon had twenty-four hour drug trafficking running out of the house. I stayed drunk and high and went without eating for days. There were also occasions when I had to threaten or injure a person for becoming unruly and out of control. I played the role of bouncer, dealer, and coke chef, not surprisingly. My life was completely out of control. I no longer felt any desire to survive and was just allowing myself to wither away to dust.

One day trafficking was slow and I was feenin for drugs. I stripped the copper pipes from the basement and sold them. I added in anything else I found around the house that was costly enough to be sold or traded.

Back in Virginia my two brothers, Tootie and Rusty, were not financially capable of keeping up with mortgage payments so the bank had begun the foreclosure process. They were working the janitorial business, but weren't seeing enough profits to pay their bills. Our oldest brother, Jr., kept us all in the dark concerning the financial aspects of the business. When I was working with them, my addiction had played a role with my irresponsibility enough to be more informed about the business aspects of the franchise. I knew things weren't being disclosed for a particular reason and I confronted my brother about it. Instead, he sucker punched me in the face in my own home, right in front of my brothers. They just sat by and watched him do it even though they also had stakes in the matter.

Jr. wasn't aware that I held a 22-caliber pistol in my bedroom and was seriously contemplating using it. That was the day I committed myself into the Tidewater Psychiatric Hospital. They sent me back to Boston. When the mortgage company finally evicted my brothers, they only packed a few of their belongings. They left the rest of our mother's mementos and furniture and went to make camp in the Virginia woods in a makeshift hut.

Tootie actually brought those filthy cats with them.

When I got word of this, I could only think about what real losers they were! Soon after the foreclosure and eviction, Rusty left Virginia Beach and showed up at the house we shared in Boston. It was crazy business as usual. Rusty never skipped a beat. He would get drunk and loud at times, especially when I had big-time drug dealers using the house to process their drugs. Enough drugs ran through the house to get us sent to prison and for our home to be forfeited.

Rusty didn't care. He acted way out of character. Yelling and screaming for no apparent reason. He just wanted to get high. He was like a dog begging for a treat. He couldn't just wait for the drug lords to handle their business and leave. To make matters worse, Rusty brought home a stray

Labrador puppy who was defecating all around the house. Now I found myself having to clean up after his untrained Mutt!

My mind went psycho. I couldn't take much more of this abuse. I went and stayed at the veteran's shelter and sometimes at our cousin's house. I had to separate myself from that situation with Rusty. When I was home, we'd argue and the neighbors would hear the loud noise emanating from our house. The neighbors would get scared and call the police. They would arrive with threats to lock both of us up if they had to return.

To avoid getting locked up I waited until Rusty fell asleep by lurking in the shadows of the dangerous streets of Boston. Every night, just like Virginia, he'd get drunk then cuss at me, then tell me that he'd be up stairs.

"Come kill me."

Once upstairs he'd continue to yell obscenities for hours until he passed out. When we both weren't drinking which was a rare occasion, I tried to reason with him. I urged that we try and get sober using the buddy system.

I loved my brother deeply with all my heart.

I knew that we were both above average intelligent men. I truly believed that we could get clean and stay sober as a team. Rusty just laughed in my face at my proposal. It was a hurtful feeling to be rejected, especially by him and especially for matters of such importance. Soon after that, I was committed back into detox at the Arbor Psychiatric Hospital in Jamaica Plain. I was so far gone that it was the only treatment center in the greater Boston area that was capable of handling a basket case like me.

I was given a sleep deprived EEG. They discovered that I had an abnormal frontal lobe, but other test results dismissed any significant mental disorders. It became obvious that the alcohol and drugs were the most contributing factor to my mental illness. The staff tried three times to send me to an extensive treatment facility. I sabotaged those attempts by picking up a drink or drug. I was also prescribed different types of anti-psychotics like Mellaril. In high doses, these medications are used to treat patients who suffer delusions. I still continued to use drugs and alcohol while on those prescribed medications. I became a walking zombie and a tragic incident waiting to happen.

I was once admitted into the psychiatric hospital with my clothes covered with blood, but no visible signs of cuts or trauma to my body. I had blacked out and forgotten where I'd been or what I'd gotten into. When no bodies showed up at the morgue, the medical staff admitted me again. This time I was admitted for one month during which time I participated in counseling, education groups, and attend NA/AA meetings. I was never able to procure a sponsor, not even on a temporary basis. I was too proud to ask for help and still believed I could do this on my own. Eventually, I was released back into the wild without any kind of support system.

The entire time I was out there in the streets, I never forgot about my wife and children. I believed that somehow it was imperative for me to get my life on track so I could reach out to them. I knew they needed me and I needed them as well. The thought of my daughters growing up resenting me really gave me the will and desire to continue fighting for my life. I refused to let them go through life thinking I didn't love them as my father sometimes led me to believe. Crucial time was wasting while my mind, body, and soul were slowly rotting away.

Even the psychiatrist was stopped at a crossroad with me. In order for them to effectively treat me, I needed to first get myself clean and sober. All the hurt I had been subjected to in my life compounded by all the hurt I caused along with the drinking and drugs made me a very sick person. I went back home to the crack den and during the next three months my nose was broken, busted lips, robbed, shot at, beat up, and forced to slice up a couple of fellas. I also got arrested for disturbing the peace while arguing with Rusty.

Each night I'd leave out my house to hustle, something terrible would transpire. For protection I began leaving the house carrying multiple weapons such as a butcher knife, screw driver, box cutter or ice pick. Later I'd arrive home bloody sometimes with a fist full of dollars. I wouldn't even remember or care about the responsibilities that might be forth coming. The last thing I needed after barely making it home from a street battle was to enter another battle with

Rusty. It was as if he waited up for me to come home.

"Where you been?"

"What you got?"

"What have you been doing?"

He'd ask before demanding half of my treasures. He'd state that everything that enters this house was half his. One night I came close to being injured, just to get away with forty dollars worth of crack. My brother and I got into a disagreement over what portion of my stolen treasure that he was going to receive. Rusty got angry, swiped my drugs off the kitchen counter, and the package landed in the wet sink and dissolved.

That was it for me.

I hurried and left that house out of fear of hurting him. The next day I phoned our father. I begged and pleaded with him to come intervene in this matter before somebody got seriously hurt. I explained the entire dreadful situation to him and he promised to stop by after work. Two days passed but our father never showed up.

A few evenings later, I was sitting at home in the kitchen around eleven o'clock. I was feenin and scraping resins of cocaine off a plate trying to get high. Rusty enters the house and begins yelling and screaming for no apparent reason. He had just left the neighborhood bar where he had been drinking. I tried to ignore him but he kept walking up to me, taunting and pointing in my face, and repeatedly called me his "bitch".

Finally, he walked up the stairs to his second floor bedroom. I was relieved because I thought that he was going up there to sleep it off. Instead, Rusty quickly returned carrying a large stick which he used to poke me. He knocked the plate with the cocaine resin on the floor. I just sat there as I wondered why my brother was treating me this way. Suddenly, Rusty screamed at me.

"Stop crying, you faggot bitch"

Then he started bashing me in the face and head with the stick knocking me off my seat.

Rusty surprised me. He's never attacked me like this before. My head hurt and blood was seeping out my mouth. I was in shock. In a flash response to being attacked so violently, I grabbed a steak knife out of the sink and stabbed my brother once in the chest. Rusty gasped and then collapsed to the orange-tiled floor.

After checking and seeing he was hurt really bad, I ran next door and ask the neighbors to call for an ambulance. Afterwards I hurried back to my brother and applied first-aid to his wound. That moment I looked at him. I saw an unforgettable distant glare in his eyes. It caused me to clutch him close.

"Hold on Rusty!" I pleaded.

The medical emergency response team arrived with the Boston police. They saw me holding my brothers limp body in my arms. I was handcuffed and immediately place under arrest and taken to the police station. While I was being booked for assault and battery with a dangerous weapon, the telephone rang and was answered by the desk sergeant. The sergeant suddenly ordered the booking officer to upgrade the charges to murder; *Murder in the first-degree!*

This news initially did not register in my brain. I felt numb and did not understand what it meant – Murder in the first degree - .

Then there came a brief period of relief. I knew that this hellish nightmare was finally over. I won't be going through any of that physical and mental agony anymore.

I felt the full effect of the news and I cried my brother's name out loud,

"Rusty!"

"Rusty!"

"Rusty!"

When my brother died a large portion of me followed him to his grave. The last time I took a drink or drug was July 30, 1996.

It was a bitter sweet moment with no cause for jubilant celebrations.

I, Stone, had finally reached that abysmal rock bottom.

Sobriety   by
                                              Stone 04

Chapter

Nine

SOBRIETY

I was allowed to make one phone call immediately after being booked and finger printed. I used it to call my father to inform him of this tragic and devastating news. The phone rang four times before I heard his mild-toned voice,

"Hello, Dad."

"Rusty's dead."

"I killed him," I cried!

Nothing but silence came from the other end of the phone. Then I said, "Sorry dad, I didn't mean it."

I handed the receiver to the booking officer and was locked in a jail cell containing a concrete slab for a bed and stainless steel toilet and sink. I lay awake throughout the night sobbing for the loss of my brother Rusty. I never meant for him to die. I was missing him already. I knew that many other people, family, and friends would not only miss him, but they would be angry at me. I had stabbed him to death.

With my reputation, no one would believe what led to the incident.

The next morning I was arraigned at the Dorchester District Courthouse where I was formally charged with the first-degree murder of my brother. A charge of first-degree murder in the Commonwealth of Massachusetts carries a sentence of life in prison without the possibility of parole! Handcuffed and barefoot, I was escorted into the courtroom wearing a pair of dirty dungaree shorts and ripped up bloody white t-shirt. Both my lips and one eye were almost swollen shut. Dried blood caked my face.

This particular morning, there was a large audience presence in the courtroom. I glanced into the crowd from the docket booth and noticed my father and cousin standing there appearing disturbed and confused. At that moment, all I could do was stare at my father with tears flowing down my cheek. I shrugged my shoulder to say ' I don't know what happened.'

Please save me!

A not guilty plea was entered on my behalf by a court appointed attorney who was assigned by the court to represent me.

Afterwards, I was quickly ushered back into the holding tank, better known as the bull pen, which this morning was non-surprisingly full with men. Men who, like myself, had been arrested the night before. Moments after, I was locked into the bull pen, I saw an old school friend of mine. I called her 'Kool-aid' because of her big cheery smile and overall sweetness. She worked at the courthouse as a clerk. She was passing through the halls on her way to make a delivery when I called out,

"Hey Kool-aid!"

She instantly recognized me and approached the bull pen screen to say hello and asked me what was up. I explained my tragic situation, as briefly as I could, as if she could just go convince the judge that this was all a misunderstanding, and then he would release me.

"For God's sake," I cried. "He was my brother!"

Kool-aid looked me over then momentarily excused herself. She returned a short time later carrying some items in her hands. Through the bars of the cage, she handed me a clean t-shirt, shower slippers, a pack of cigarettes, and a lighter. She asked me if there was anyone that I needed for her to contact. At that instant, I thought of my two young daughters, but I told her no.

Kool-aid gave her condolences to my family and I thanked her before she had to head back to work. I sat on a cold slab of concrete, chain smoking for three hours. The police escorts arrived to transfer me and others to the county jail where I was held waiting a trial date. Bail was set so high that I remained at the county jail for about eighteen months before being sentenced to sixteen years in the state prison system.

During my time at the county jail, I was visited by my big brother Jr. and his son. My sister Greta brought my then young nephew. It was only my second time ever seeing him. The first was at my mother's funeral and it made me sad to have him see me, his emaciated crack crazed uncle, under these circumstances.

The treatment I endured at the county jail while waiting for trial was horrendous. I was locked in a segregated unit. Besides my cell there were thirty-three other cells occupied by men who were also awaiting trial - all facing murder charges.

It was considered a high-risk unit, so we were not allowed out of the unit to participate in any educational or substance abuse groups. The only support I had to help get me through this painful experience was the spiritual support of my aunt and grandmother. They both insisted that I call them at least once or twice a week.

My aunt introduced me to Bible scriptures and taught me how to pray over the phone. Her spiritual guidance truly helped to sustain me through this tough time. I was living in the small confines of a very strenuous, untamed environment with drug dealers and addicts, like myself, who were using and gang bangers. They were constantly doing battle over control of the unit. I had plenty of opportunity to drink a batch of home brew or smoke crack but somehow I knew that the time had come for me to quit.

My brother was dead.

I killed him.

I fought to remain sober for him while searching deep within myself for the answers to all of life's little questions.

I often asked myself, "Am I really an animal?"

I was spiritually bankrupt.

My thoughts were not that of a normal, healthy human spirit. From the age of fourteen to thirty-four, I've been nothing but an outcast to myself and my family. Every night in my lonely jail cage, full of demons, I dreamt of getting high. I could actually taste and feel the substance enter my bloodstream and transport me to another galaxy. At this late stage, my addiction had taken everything I had - family, friends, my freedom, and the *life* of my closest brother. I had forfeited two homes and cars. All my material possessions were gone. There was nothing left for me to give to my addiction.

I truly and finally had reached my rock bottom.

Each day, I mailed out letters to family members and friends attempting to apologize for my wrongful actions, but none of them were ever answered. I became emotionally depressed and thought about taking my own life. By this time, I had been convicted and transferred to state prison at MCI-Concord, a maximum security facility. At the time, Concord was being used as a classification-phase prison until my transfer to where I would be serving most of my time.

The prison atmosphere feels angry, cold and extremely unforgiving. Initially, I had to carry a weapon for protection. Not only was violent and sexual danger always lurking about but I began running into men who've been waiting for many years to finally cross my path. Within four months of being housed in state prison, I thought what the heck was I doing this time for? I've lost everything and everybody, and by the time I get out, if I indeed make it out, I'll be an unhealthy, bitter old man.

I grew increasingly depressed and the suicidal ideas became stronger and more frequent.

Just when I reached the threshold of my breaking point, with one foot in the grave, I received a letter from my youngest daughter Trudy, who was about fourteen years old at that time. In her youthful, neat handwriting, she wrote to inform me that her grandmother, Donna, my wife's mother, had passed away.

In spite of everything that she knew, heard or felt about me, she forgave me.

Trudy ended her letter by stating how much she loved me. If it was okay with me, she would like to continue to correspond. My daughter's letter penetrated to the depths of my heart. Her presence in my life rejuvenated my spirit. She was an angel sent from heaven who brought new and colorful meaning to my daunted life. Her words sweetened up the salty tears I cried each day. They transformed my sadness into gladness.

Before receiving her letter, I had been attending weekly AA/NA meetings, mainly to escape the bitter confines of a lonely prison cell. I wasn't using, but my mind was stuck in remission. Looking back, it was a matter of time before I picked up again.

After my daughter's letter, I began listening and sharing my experiences in the meetings. I discovered how alive and purposeful this made me feel. When I got transferred to MCI-Norfolk, a medium-security facility, where I was able to enjoy more freedoms, I quickly joined up for the Twelve Step and Big Book study groups. Because of my commitment to these sober programs, I was voted in as secretary and treasurer.

Imagine *me,* yes me, in charge of the finances? I was a responsible and trustworthy person these days.

Suddenly I had a new lease on life and although I was locked up in prison, I wanted to live a righteous life. Yet there still seemed to be a void in my calling.

I joined the protestant church services and sang in the choir. I wore the Lord's choir robe and I felt like an Army soldier dressed for war against ungodly alcohol and drugs.

I gave all my battles to the Lord.

Turning my life over completely to God was an uplifting spiritual experience. It fully resurrected me from the living dead, like Lazarus. I was ordered by the Lord to rise up. I obeyed him and I dusted myself off and began changing my negative thought patterns to positive pro-social thoughts. Over the course of time, my eyes were completely open to the turrets and harsh realities of life. God carried me until I was able to walk.

Create in me a clean
heart, oh God;
And renew a right spirit within me.
– Psalms 52:10

I continued believing that my past life was justified up until the day when I received that spiritual awakening. The stealing, abuse, and the dishonesty towards my parents justified through my lack of knowledge and understanding, and compounded by my addiction.

This couldn't have been further from the truth.

I came to realize how most of my life I played the role of a weak, sneaky coward. Now, I believed it was time for me to rise up and atone for the sins I had committed, not just against myself, but God and also against society. It was now time for me to be a responsible man and give back what I took from my victims.

On a warm, sunny morning in July of 1999, I was baptized in the name of Jesus Christ for the first time in my life.

> Amazing grace, how sweet the sound
> That saved a wretch like me.
> I once was lost, but now I'm found
> Was blind, but now I see.

Looking back at those first sober five years while in custody, I continued to experience realistic dreams of getting high. Each time they came I would force myself out of the dream before picking up. I would jump out of bed onto my knees and prayed for my higher power to please release me from the grips of my addiction. By the seventh year, these dreams and desires had almost dissipated. I continued to strengthen my relationship with God. My daughter Trudy was writing to me at least twice a month to ask me questions about her ancestors. With what little knowledge I knew about family, it still felt good to be able to answer some of her questions.

Our correspondence was very therapeutic - for the both of us. Trudy appeared very mature for a girl her age. I attributed that to the fact that she and Elizabeth practically raised themselves with my being gone. Initially, Trudy had serious issues with my being absent from her life and she wasn't shy about speaking to me about them. Then there were moments when she became frustrated at me because I couldn't be there physically for her. Therefore, I wouldn't hear from her for a few months. She'd return with a brighter and positive attitude and outlook on things.

With her help, I've learned to live righteously through my daughter Trudy. I wished that her sister Elizabeth would cave in and contact me. But, she and their mother continue to be reluctant to allow me back into their lives. They are also at odds with Trudy for communicating with me. They had even urged her not to mention them through her letters to me.

Throughout these times, I continued to participate in recovery groups and attend church services. I began experiencing some real advanced spiritual growth. Looking back, I started drinking and drugging at the young age of fourteen and here I was at age forty-one finally becoming a mature responsible man.

'When I was a child, I spoke as a child,
I acted as a child,
But now that I am a man,
I put away childish things'.
1 Cor 13:11

With a whopping seven years clean and sober, I was able to discern right from wrong and was able to ignore emotional and sensual feelings and make intelligent decisions. I was also able to work on changing my ways of thinking negative to a more positive way of living. This required me to make a searching and fearless moral inventory of myself and for this I looked to my recovery group and sponsor for help.

With a pen and paper, I traveled back as far as my memory would allow. I conjured up all the hurtful or damaging experiences that I had endured. I wrote down all my character traits, good and bad. I took a good thorough look at myself then began the tedious task of changing my belief system. I learned that I was compulsive and anything that looked, tasted, or felt good I was capable of abusing.

Donald R. Frye

I have an addictive personality.

At one meeting, held in the prison auditorium, I put down my macho pride. As I addressed the crowd, I broke down and cried. I cried in front of two-hundred hardened convicts, most of whom were serving life sentences as a result of their own addiction issues.

I gave these men all of my pain.

I could no longer hold onto it.

It was time for me to let go and move on to a brighter future. Once again, I had seen the light to a better, sober way of living. That meeting was a liberating experience for me. It felt as if a granite building had been lifted up off me.

At that moment, I discovered that it was okay to experience pain and to cry. After that meeting, I was greeted and hugged by my sober peers, many who were just as serious about their recovery. I now realized that if I wanted to stay clean and sober, I would have to chase sobriety as hard as I chased the drink or drug.

Every word coming from my lips was AA/NA this and Jesus that. People who weren't serious about their recovery and who wished to stay stuck in the triple stages of darkness, would swiftly walk the other way when they saw little o'le me coming.

I was respecting people and people were respecting me.

My letters to my wife and daughter Elizabeth began to sound more genuinely apologetic. Then one day something special occurred. After my forty-third birthday, I received a letter in the mail from my wife Rhonda.

"I think it is time I let you back in, but just as friends," the letter stated.

I still have that letter as proof that time can heal old wounds. I was very ecstatic about these new turn of events. I believed that it would be just a matter of time before I received a similar note from my oldest daughter Elizabeth. My wife wrote me a second time to ask me why I treated her the way I did. My response, after some deep thinking, was as truthful as my heart would allow.

I did not hide behind my addiction. I took full responsibility for my actions.

I told her that I treated her bad out of fear and self-hatred. I had acted as an immature, selfish coward who tainted one of Gods most beautiful creations. I expressed how sad and truly remorseful I was for all the pain that I caused her and our children. At this stage, my wife was also in and out of recovery. After kicking me out of our home, she had continued to use since that first regretful day I introduced her to drugs in 1986. All these years she was still out there sick and suffering.

I felt that she could use my support. I extended my heart and hands out to her by mailing her some AA/NA pamphlets and other spiritual literature. I hoped that she would latch on.

"Bring the body and the mind shall follow."

Her letters have ceased, but I still feel we've reached a huge reconciliation milestone; just by her writing at all.

Prison with its deplorable living conditions is a very strenuous unforgiving chamber of pain.

In here, I'm constantly being deprived and harassed by racist prison officials. I'm barraged with inmate psycho-babble; some are always trying to get over on anything they can. I persevere on life's terms, without the use of a drink or drug.

"One day, one moment, at a time"

Life is still difficult. Sometimes, I become overburden and feel like giving up but that's when I holler out loud singing the Lord's Prayer. I practice the spiritual principles taught to me in my sober circles, and that's how I get by and keep my sanity. I'm constantly on alert for my triggers. Triggers such as: being around people who use, idle time, money, depression, bad relationships, and the frustration of not having things turn out the way I want them to.

The education I received throughout the years from the Correctional recovery programs has helped me understand that my addiction is very angry at me for neglecting it for so long. My addiction is lurking and prepared to strike at any moment of weakness. It could easily pull me back into its grips.

Donald R. Frye

Today, I do not have any desires to pick up a drink or drug, nor do I have any future reservations. I'm happy to be able to experience the pains and joys of life and to deal with them positively like a real man. For instance, I continue to witness and experience the prejudices, greed, poverty, and violence of this world.

Today, I don't drink or drug over these things like I use to. I even get the urge to steal or cheat, but I don't because that may lead me back to using.

My plans are to continue to educate myself through my participation in recovery programs. I plan to apply what I've learned to help keep me clean and sober. I also plan to make amends to those I've hurt.

Today, for me, sobriety comes first.

Just like when I placed drugs and alcohol above all else. Sobriety is my new and healthy vice and I'm loving it. I invite everyone, addicts and families of addicts, to this festive moment of living life on life's terms without the use of alcohol or drugs.

It wasn't easy for me, but as time passed and I kept going to those meetings and surrounded myself with sober people who were doing positive things, I am able to walk confidently while never having to peak over my shoulder.

I'm extremely remorseful and sad that my journey ended on such a tragic and hurtful note. I know that it's okay for me to experience these pains of the past. I know I have family and good friends that I can confide in.

God willing, I will be released from prison in mid 2010, so I look forward to meeting up with you in the recovery halls. You'll never have to go through what I went through if you just keep coming back!

It works if you work it.

Donald R. Frye

conscientious

Stone '0?

Summary

CONSCIENTIOUS

I was raised in a single-parent home. My family resided in a poverty stricken neighborhood where I was subjected to physical, sexual and emotional abuse. Sadly these behaviors are most prevalent in the ghetto. I am able to recall many times when I was subjected to unprovoked physical or emotionally charged acts that to this day can hold me crippled in fear.

During these times, I hid my fears. A man or boy like me is not supposed to display any signs of fear, because to my peers, it meant a sign of weakness. Scared boys were treated with disrespect or made fun of. I was taught to be strong so I did my best to conceal my fears. I concealed my fears being better than my peers at things such as sports or relationships. I would convince girls to have sexual intercourse with me. I'd also do other negative things that some of the tougher crowds in the ghetto would do such a consistent truancy and take property that didn't belong to me.

At a young age, instead of hanging in the treacherous streets, I joined the Roxbury Boys Club where I began spending most of my time after school. My instincts warned me that the more time I spent in the streets, the more likely I'd end up injured and arrested for breaking the law.

Looking back, I believe that I was acting smart by playing it safe and joining the Boy's club. While spending time there I only had to prove my worth by being the best at games and sports. On the streets I proved myself by risking being hurt or hurting others, breaking the law, and landing myself in jail. Although I did enjoy the competitive environment in sports, I still continued to feel fearful of life. I did what I thought I had to do to conceal it.

I learned from television shows like Return of the Mack, and Superfly, which portrayed black characters as pimps, pushers, and street hustlers, that by having the most pussy, money, or material things, that I could improve my status amongst my peers. I did these things to make me feel superior, which easily helped me to conceal and escape my fears.

With my high status with the "in" crowd, I found myself being feared by some. I had the reputation of the kid who disobeyed authority. I took risks stealing the things that my parents weren't able to afford.

I stole designer clothes, footwear, bicycles, electronics and other gadgets. I also manipulated the girls who I went out with into furnishing me with the things I thought I needed to uphold my image, even if it meant for them to steal, manipulate or prostitute themselves.

The release I experienced during unprotected sexual relationships with many different females helped to relieve the stress caused by my fears. Even though I was aware of the consequences of being promiscuous, I continued to use girls for sexual pleasure. In my mind the risk of exposing my fears outweighed the risk or hurting someone's feelings, catching a communicable disease or even worse, being sent to jail, something I feared very much. I was caught up in a catch-22.

Throughout the years I learned that I used negative things like drinking and drugs to hide my fears but they actually increased my fears to a point that I grew impulsive, anxious, and insecure about myself, but by then, I was addicted to the substances. By the time I reached the age of fourteen, I had become indoctrinated into the sub-culture, or life, of the substance abuser.

Donald R. Frye

The sub-culture, or life, of the substance abuser, is a leading cause of the moral, economic, and spiritual breakdown of families and entire communities. These sub-cultures render the inhabitants unable or unwilling to unite or cope with the progression and defense of the society in which they reside. The inhabitant's primary objective, it seems, is to escape reality through the consumption of alcohol or drugs. Satisfying their addictions comes at a huge sacrifice to families with children, many who are born out of wedlock to single parents.

These children are often abused, neglected, and left to fend for themselves. The numbers are staggering. There is an old adage that reads, "When man is taken from the home - physically, mentally, or spiritually - the women will stray and the children rebel."

They are believed to rebel by acting out at home, school, or society. Children will turn to resentful or destructive acts and are prone to join gangs for protection and support. Gangs are led by members who violently claim and defend their "turf."

This turf is where they indulge in selling and experimenting with alcohol and drugs, unsafe sex, or prostitution. Thus perpetuating the vicious cycle initiated by their guardians which depreciates the oral economic value of the community.

Today, a family or community living in such a poor and confused state is prone to be easily controlled or manipulated by the media, bankers, politicians, civic leaders, jailers, developers, organized crime, and others. They have an economic interest in either the upkeep or demise of such a moral-less society.

It is a well documented fact that the European settlers introduced alcohol to the native Indians. The native's consumption of alcohol contributed with curtailing their efforts to defend their land. It is also well documented that alcohol and heroin was introduced into the black community as a contributing weapon to dismantle the civil rights movement and to oppress them. The consumption of heroin and its effect on the wars caused over control of the heroin market. It rendered it impossible for the black community to unify and carry out its own agenda.

Donald R. Frye

As a substance abuser, who for twenty-years during my usage, I managed to survive the self-inflicted torture and destruction of my family and community, only to deliver this critical message of unnecessary human suffering to all readers.

I hope taking you through my life of addiction and recovery from alcohol and drugs touches the hearts and minds of the many cultures of men, women, and children out there in this world. Those who are suffering from a dreadful disease of addiction, but thought that they were alone. You are not alone, I am right here with you. And as you now come to know that we have sometimes traveled down those same dangerous, unpredictable, and regretful roads while feeding our addictions. We neglected ourselves, loved ones, and friends while under the influence of alcohol and drugs.

Now it is time that we travel together on those same roads to recovery. It will lead us to a safe, sober, and productive life, today and forevermore, one day, or moment at a time.

It was with extensive thought and deep emotional reward that I made this conscious choice to share my story with the entire world. I truly believe that this represents my willingness and strong desire to stay clean and sober and help others achieve sobriety. I confess that it was an extremely difficult decision because I was afraid that I'd be risking my relationships with people I love. Those whom never seen or heard about the depths of despair that my addiction brought me to. They will definitely view me in a different light, but some might shut the door on our relationship, and that's okay for me today.

Liberating myself supersedes the aspects of others. So, in order for me to completely liberate myself I had to take those risks and get this story out there to you. Initially, for me to get sober and stay sober, my soul needed cleansing. It then needed to be filled with new edifying and nourishing knowledge. All which I acquired throughout the years while attending recovery programs, self-help groups, help from sponsors, and meetings. It was just as important for me to apply this knowledge which is what helped me change my old criminal thinking and impulsive behaviors to positive, constructive and pro-social methods of a new life.

In my travels, I've discovered that I was as sick as some of my secrets and that freedom initially starts from within. Once I was released from the bondage of my inner self, then I became exposed to an entirely new healthy world. I confronted those dark secrets and learned how to deal with them on life's terms without the use of drinks or drugs. I've learned to forgive the people, places, or things in my life that I felt were keeping me in bondage. I forgave myself for the wrongs I've committed while trying throughout the years to evade or suppress that which kept me sick. Now in the memorable words of the late Dr. Martin Luther King, Jr.:

"Free at Last. Free at Last. Thank God Almighty, I'm free at last!"

IN REMEMBERANCE OF
RAMON 'RUSTY' G. FRYE
August 10, 1960 – July 30, 1996

My brother Ramon (Rusty), God rest his soul, was the second youngest of five siblings. I was the youngest. We were two years apart, but our close size and resemblance led others to believe that we were twins. We were closer to each other than our other siblings. We could always be seen traveling together to and from grade school, having fun at the Roxbury Boys & Girls Club of Boston's game rooms, gym, or swimming pool.

At an early age, we were being groomed by our swim coach, our dad, to become the first African-American competitive swimmers and divers from the city of Boston and the Commonwealth of Massachusetts. With the backing of proud confident sponsors who lent their prestige, finances, and time for us to practice the sport, we competed and won many first prize awards in the Boys Clubs of America, Amateur Athletic Union (AAU), and other New England states swimming and diving events. We also performed together in exhibition diving events, television commercials, and the Sparky the Fire Dog's "Learn-Not-To-Burn" campaign. Rusty also made cameo appearances on Jabberwocky, a WGBH sponsored kid's television program. He also served four years in the United States Air Force.

Rusty was my inseparable companion who shared my clothes, bath, food, and bed. I love and miss him dearly. When he left us, a huge part of me followed, but at the same token a huge part of him remained.

May my brother, Ramon, rest in peace knowing that we all love and miss him. Surviving him is his beautiful daughter, Echo, and granddaughter, Azure.

Ramon Garfield Frye

August 10,1960 – July 30, 1996

More books from Donald Frye (Stone) coming soon. To order additional copies of this book, any of his drawings or any TJG Management published books go to:

www.tjgstore.com

This book is also available on Amazon and in Kindle format.

SIT BACK, RELAX AND READ!